M**O**NEY
MADE EASY
2015-16

Every owner of a physical copy of

Money Made Easy 2015–16

can download the eBook for free direct from us at Harriman House, in a DRM-free format that can be read on any eReader, tablet or smartphone.

Simply head to:

ebooks.harriman-house.com/moneymadeeasy

to get your copy now.

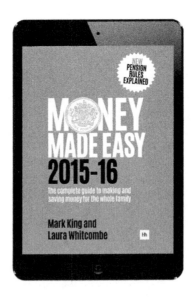

MONEY MADE EASY 2015-16

The complete guide to making and saving money for the whole family

MARK KING
& LAURA WHITCOMBE

MT

HARRIMAN HOUSE LTD
18 College Street
Petersfield
Hampshire
GU31 4AD
GREAT BRITAIN
Tel: +44 (0)1730 233870

Email: **enquiries@harriman-house.com**
Website: **www.harriman-house.com**

First published in Great Britain in 2015.

Paperback ISBN: 978-0-85719-490-9
eBook ISBN: 978-0-85719-492-3

British Library Cataloguing in Publication Data
A CIP catalogue record for this book can be obtained from the British Library.

Design: Mark Stammers

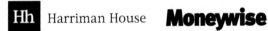 

7/5/16

About the authors

Mark King is an award-winning personal finance journalist and editor. He spent more than 16 years at the *Guardian* and *Observer* writing on personal finance and investment issues. He is now editor of *Moneywise* magazine and website and regularly appears on BBC Radio. Mark has been shortlisted for an award at the 2015 Headline Money Awards, which recognise the work of financial journalists.

Laura Whitcombe is a personal finance journalist and the deputy editor of *Moneywise* magazine and website. She is a contributor to *Spectator Money* and has also written for *The Spectator* and *Money Observer*. She is also a personal finance commentator appearing regularly on BBC radio and TV. Laura has been shortlisted for an award at the 2015 Headline Money Awards, which recognise the work of financial journalists.

Foreword

We all crave financial security – whether it's as a newly-wed joyously starting a family, or as someone looking to enjoy retirement after a working life of hard graft and saving.

Financial security doesn't come easy (I know from personal experience!). In fact, it's probably harder than ever given a fluid employment market (zero-hour contracts and all that), the continued difficulty many people have in jumping onto the housing ladder, and mountainous student debts (my three boys are currently submerged in them).

And, of course, we have a welfare state that continues to draw back. Financial help from the government still exists but it's increasingly in short supply.

Yet a little financial discipline can go a long way in building the foundations for financial security. And although the state may not be giving money away as generously as it once did (in the form of benefits) it continues to encourage individual financial empowerment. It does this through tax incentives on savings and help for first-time homebuyers.

For those who want to become financially empowered, I can think of no better starting point than reading this splendid book. Cutting through the jargon that plagues money matters, it will arm you with all the information necessary to tackle the financial jungle.

Whether it's how to make money, save money, protect your family financially against illness or death (sorry to mention that horrible word) or how to best use your savings in retirement in light of the new pension freedom rules, this essential financial book provides the answers.

Enjoy the read (I did). If it helps you on your journey to financial security, then the book will have served its purpose. And, of course, I will be overjoyed.

Jeff Prestridge
Personal Finance Editor
The Mail on Sunday

Contents

Introduction

Money Made Easy 2015–16 is here to help you master your personal finances. We'll cut through the jargon and explain clever but simple ways to make and save money.

The good news is that whatever age you are, however much you earn, whatever your history, you can always improve your financial position by getting organised. You don't need a new job or a pay rise; you can improve your finances without making any major lifestyle changes – and you can do it today.

After all, we make decisions about money every day. Some are more obvious than others. Putting your house up for sale and moving elsewhere, for example, will have a major impact on your finances. But the consequences of, say, sticking with a credit card that no longer offers interest-free purchases can quickly become significant too, even if we do overlook the importance.

In the past few years alone, we've bought, sold and altered property, embarked on a buy-to-let adventure, helped our own parents financially, got married, and had children – and that's just the big things. As financial journalists, we're also mindful of the day-to-day need to keep our finances fit, from checking the rate on our cash savings to picking the best home and travel insurance policies and even keeping our shopping bills down. Without a decent working knowledge of personal finance, all of this would be a lot harder – not to mention financially draining.

That's why, through this book, we want to help take you on a financial journey that you can use at every stage of your life, so you'll have the tools at your disposal to ensure you always get a good deal, however old you are.

We start off with ways to make money – but don't expect to find a long list of hair-brained, get-rich-quick schemes. Instead, we focus on sensible and realistic ways to grow your money over the long term. Our first two chapters may be concerned with investing and retirement and pensions – not the sexiest topics on Earth – but the sooner you get started with these, the more money you stand to make and the better your family's financial future could be.

This is even more crucial now the government has allowed retirees to take control of their pension in a way previous generations were denied. But with power and freedom comes responsibility, meaning retirees face tough choices about what to do with their pension. In this book, we've included all the latest on the new pension rules and how you can use them to your advantage to ensure you generate a decent income in retirement and continue living a comfortable life.

You'll also find tips on starting a business in our Make Money section, from where to find start-up funding to what to include in your business plan.

We couldn't omit property from our Make Money section. While a house should always be a home rather than anything else, over time we all hope our property's value will increase and add to our overall wealth. That's why we've dedicated a chapter to how to buy and sell property. While some of the information will be more relevant to first-timers, there's still plenty of useful stuff for those buying or selling for the second, third, or even tenth time. We outline all you need to know about the different types of mortgage available, a rundown of the government's Help to Buy scheme – including the introduction of Help to Buy Isas – and the new Stamp Duty regimes across the UK and Scotland.

To make serious money, you need to be in the best financial shape possible at any given time. This involves getting rid of expensive debt, cutting unnecessary spending and building up your savings, which is why these three issues form the basis of our second section: Save Money.

Sadly, people fall on hard times – often through no fault of their own, such as redundancy or ill health. In these situations, repaying debt can prove difficult, and interest and late charges can start to mount up. But in Save Money we'll teach you to tackle your debt – whether you owe £100 or £100,000 – and help put you on a path to becoming debt-free.

As for cutting unnecessary spending, we'll give you the tools you need to budget effectively and get the very most out of every pound you spend – from cashback to loyalty card schemes.

We round off the Save Money section by covering savings goals and detailing practical ways to build up a significant savings pot you'll be able to spend on things such as holidays, a new car or even a wedding. You may not think you can afford to save, but we'll show you just how easy it can be.

We've devoted another section to getting organised for life's big events – and preparing for the unexpected. From a practical guide to getting married and merging your finances with those of another, to having children and arranging insurance, we'll give you the tools you need to protect your family. We'll also walk you through the divorce process and explain how joint finances can be untangled. And looking to the (hopefully) very distant future, we also take you through the importance of setting up a will and keeping it up to date, plus the essentials of estate planning.

We've also put together a useful product guide covering the very building blocks of personal finance, to help you get your head around the myriad things your financial providers might try to flog to you. We'll talk you through current and savings accounts, teach you the difference between building societies and banks, and why you need to know how easy-access savings differ from fixed-rate bonds.

In a similar vein, you'll also find a jargon buster at the back of the book that you'll be able to refer to any time your financial providers try to bamboozle you.

Once you've got your head around the basics, you'll be armed with the knowledge you need to start making really smart financial choices. *With Money Made Easy 2015–16*, there's no excuse not to refocus your finances, whether you're in your 20s or your 80s. It's never too late to do something that will improve your financial health. Whether you read it from start to finish, or dip in and out of chapters as you move through life, we hope this remains an invaluable guide to improving your finances.

Try to remember: personal finance is not impossible to understand; it's just a subject many people avoid. Don't be one of them. Dive in and start smartening your finances.

Good luck.

Mark King & Laura Whitcombe

PART 1:
Make Money

Investing

We all dream of being able to make money overnight. And there certainly are plenty of get-rich-quick schemes out there – the vast majority of them at best completely useless and at worst dangerous scams. However, over the long term, there's a far better way to make money. It's entirely realistic, too. It's called investment. If you have a little cash tucked away and are comfortable with taking some risk, you could be handsomely rewarded.

Of course, investing to secure a healthy financial future for yourself and your family can be a daunting challenge. The nature of stock market investment is speculative. There are no guarantees and it's entirely possible that you could lose some money, particularly over the short term. But the reward of taking such risk is the potential to generate a far better return on your money than can ever be made from leaving your cash sitting in a long-term savings account. The Association of Investment Companies says paying £50 a month into the average investment company – a type of investment you'll hear more about later – would have generated £27,734 over the past 18 years. If you'd put the same amount in savings, your £10,800 total deposit would have grown to just £12,684.

As ever, knowledge is power, and learning about financial products, risk and reward can help even the most timid investor to make informed investment decisions. But it's not easy: there are thousands of different investment products, from shares and funds to high-risk derivatives and commodities. The key to making money and unlocking this complex world is education.

Every investor is different. Some start at an early age, while others come into money later in life. Some investors wish to squirrel away small, regular amounts; others have lump sums to invest.

Whatever their background and whatever their circumstances, canny investors know exactly how much risk they are prepared to take to get the return they desire from their investments.

Smart investors will also analyse their attitude to risk as they mature because the investment decisions we make when we are younger are often very different from those we make when we are older.

In this chapter, we will help you evaluate your attitude to risk and explain the many assets available to those who dabble in the stock market, how to invest and what it will cost you.

Risk and reward

Before doing anything, beginner investors need to think hard about whether they are prepared to take on the added risk that comes with investing in anything that's not a bank or building society savings account.

Most of us start off by using a current account and it's simple: our salary gets paid in and all our bills and living expenses come out. When we're in a position to begin saving, we open a savings account or cash Isa and watch our hard-earned cash build up.

The problem with savings accounts is that while they are relatively risk-free, they do not pay a lot of interest on your money. At the time of writing, you'd have been lucky to get 2% on your savings.

In order to get a better return, people have to take on more risk. This is known as 'risk and reward': the more risk you are prepared to take, the bigger your potential reward.

Here's a good way to think about it. Are you prepared to lose any of your money, either tomorrow or in ten years' time?

If the answer is 'no', then you might not be ready to begin investing in other assets. You should continue to place your money in high-street savings accounts.

If you are prepared to see your cash (known in the investing world as 'capital') fall and rise at any point, then you're probably ready to leap into the investment arena.

In order to do so, you'll need to consider what type of investor you are, why you are investing, how long you are able to invest for and how much you are prepared to lose. Only by answering these questions will you be able to move forward.

Time frame

As a general rule, advisers recommend that if you are investing over a short time period, certainly less than five years, but usually ten years, you should stick to cash. This is because stock markets and investment assets can rise and fall in value frequently – sometimes during a single day – so if you invest for shorter time periods, you run the risk of your asset falling in value at the exact time you wish to sell it.

But if you invest for, say, 20 years, the (usually) upward momentum of the stock market over time should smooth out the peaks and troughs of this volatility and result in your investment appreciating nicely by the time you are ready to sell. But remember: nothing is ever guaranteed with the stock market.

What we do know is that, over the long term, shares tend to outperform the interest you'll earn from a savings account (cash). For example, if you invested £100 in the stock market in the 20 years to 1 May 2013, it would be worth £258 today, compared to just £118 if you'd opted for a standard bank or building society savings account.

So the longer you have to invest, the more risk you can afford to take. This is why many people saving for retirement over, say, 25 or 35 years will often invest in higher-risk shares and funds. It's also why, when they get closer to their retirement date, they will switch out of higher-risk assets and into much safer ones.

So you must think hard about why you want to invest in the first place and how long you need to reach that goal.

Spreading risk

Even if you can afford to take on a degree of risk, you'd be foolish not to try to spread this risk as much as possible. This is why the most sensible investors will ensure they have different shares (known as 'equities') representing different sectors in their portfolio. They will add collective funds, bonds and even property to try to spread the risk. And they will make sure they have assets that hail from (or invest in) different countries.

It's an approach called 'not putting all your eggs in one basket'.

So if your investment in, say, Barclays shares plummets in value, your investments in other companies may help prop up that failure and generate enough of a return to see your portfolio emerge strongly.

Indeed, research has found that asset allocation – the practice of dividing your investment portfolio among different assets such as cash, equities, bonds and property – is the key to investment success. The theory is that you can lessen the risk because each asset class will perform in a different way to others – rising when others are falling, for example. At a time when the stock market begins to fall, commercial property may begin generating above-average returns.

Typical assets you can invest in

When people think of the stock market, they tend to think of stocks and shares, even if they have no idea what they are. However, there are lots of things you can invest in via a stock exchange, either directly or indirectly. Here are some of the main types of asset you'll see discussed.

1. Cash

Cash is not only the notes and coins rattling around in your pockets and wallets; it also refers to any cash holding in a savings or current account. Even the professionals can keep investors' money in cash if they want some part of their portfolio to remain relatively risk-free.

While a bank or building society could, in theory, fail, the Financial Services Compensation Scheme (FSCS) guarantees £85,000 per person, per authorised bank or building society. This makes cash far safer than shares but because the return (or interest) on cash is so low, it means your money runs the risk of being eroded by inflation.

For example, if inflation is 2.7% and your interest rate is paying only 2%, your cash, in real terms, is worth less at the end of that year.

2. Equities

Shares or equities are simply a stake in a company. If the company does well, the share price is likely to rise and you may be able to sell the shares at a profit. But equally, if the share price falls, you could lose out. This makes equities a far riskier asset than cash.

As well as making a profit when the share price rises, some companies also pay a dividend to their shareholders, making them a useful asset for those looking to derive an income from their investment.

Equities can be bought and sold on stock exchanges around the world, from the more developed markets of the UK, US, Europe and Japan to developing markets such as Brazil, Russia, India and China.

In the UK, the main stock market is the London Stock Exchange (LSE), which is split into different indices – the most famous being the FTSE 100, comprising the largest 100 UK companies. Other well-known indices include the FTSE 250, the FTSE Fledgling and the Alternative Investment Market (AIM), though the latter lists very high-risk small and venture-capital-backed companies.

The price of a share is not just affected by how that particular company is performing; it can also be affected by wider UK and global issues, such as unemployment, political crises and even the weather. If you've invested in an ice-cream manufacturer, for example, and the next summer is a washout, you can expect your company to sell fewer ice creams, the company to make less profit and its share price to fall as a result. In this example, the company's products are as good as they ever were but circumstances beyond its control mean that shareholders still lose out (in the short term, at least – who knows what the weather will be like the following summer).

However, because equities have the potential to deliver a generous return to investors, they remain a popular choice of asset for most investors looking to invest for the long term.

3. Bonds

Bonds are loans to companies, local authorities or the government. You lend your money and are paid interest in return. They usually pay a fixed rate of interest each year (known as the 'coupon') and aim to pay back the capital at the end of a stated period (known as the 'maturity date'). This is why bonds are sometimes referred to as 'fixed interest'.

Corporate bonds are issued by companies such as Tesco and BT as a way of raising money to invest in their business. Government bonds are issued by (you guessed it) a government – in the UK these are known as 'gilts'. Once a bond has been issued, it can be traded on a stock exchange, where the price will rise or fall based on supply and demand; it can also be influenced by the wider interest-rate trend.

You will usually receive more interest from institutions that are less creditworthy, reflecting the higher risk that they might not pay you back. The amount of interest a bond or gilt pays is fixed, which means that if interest rates fall, they become more attractive; if interest rates rise, they become less attractive.

4. Property

Investors can buy a property themselves and let it out – known as 'buy to let' – or they can invest in commercial property such as shops, offices and industrial warehouses. The latter type is usually accessed via a collective fund of some type (see page 15) rather than directly, and investors benefit from rental income and the price of the property itself should it rise in value.

Commercial property is very different from residential property (the house we buy, sell and live in) and does not always rise and fall in line with residential property market movements. The value of the property itself could fall in value, while buildings might remain empty, meaning there will be no commercial tenants to pay rent. Moreover, commercial property is not a 'liquid' investment, meaning it can be difficult to buy and sell it quickly and easily.

However, many investors like to include some property in their portfolio because it helps them to diversify. For example, investors might still receive rental income even if equity dividends fall and vice versa.

Isas

An individual savings account (Isa) is a wrapper around a savings account or investment that has tax advantages. There are two types: a cash Isa and a stocks-and-shares Isa. (Cash Isas are discussed in detail on page 91.)

What is a stocks-and-shares Isa?

A stocks-and-shares Isa is a stock market-linked investment, where you wrap your tax-efficient Isa around an investment product such as shares, bonds, funds or investment trusts (see page 15 for more on funds and investment trusts). As we have seen above, investments can go down as well as up, meaning you could lose money. This is why they are better suited to longer-term investors.

How much can I put in an Isa?

Every tax year, you are entitled to a new Isa allowance. For 2015/16, this is £15,240. You can now invest the whole amount in a stocks-and-shares Isa or you can split the full amount between a stocks-and-shares Isa and a cash Isa in any combination you wish.

What are the tax advantages?

Any profits you make on a stocks-and-shares Isa are free of capital gains tax. With cash Isas, you pay no tax on savings account interest and with a stocks-and-shares Isa you don't pay tax on interest earned from bonds. This means that if you have to complete a tax return, you don't have to declare any Isa interest or profits.

However, any income (in the form of dividends) generated by shares held within a stocks-and-shares Isa are subject to a 10% tax, which is already deducted and can't be reclaimed.

This means that, while higher- and additional-rate taxpayers are better off in an Isa (as they would otherwise pay 32.5% or 42.5% respectively), basic-rate taxpayers would receive exactly the same amount of money whether their investment were inside or outside the Isa wrapper.

MONEY MADE EASY 2015-16

What charges will I pay?

Charges on stocks-and-shares Isas depend on your choice of account and how you invest the money. While you may be hit with an initial and an annual charge of between 0.5% and 5.5% on a fund-based Isa, if you have a self-select Isa (where you choose the assets you want to hold, rather than a fund manager making the decisions for you) you could face dealing charges and stamp duty on shares and an annual plan fee.

Can I transfer one Isa to another?

Yes, but you must stick to the rules. The simplest way to transfer is to ask your new Isa manager to do it for you. You'll need to complete an application form to open the new Isa, as well as a transfer request form. The new provider will then contact your existing Isa manager and arrange for the funds to be transferred to your new one.

You are also now able to transfer between the cash and stocks-and-shares versions of Isas.

Who can have an Isa?

Any UK resident can open a cash Isa from the age of 16 and a stocks-and-shares Isa from the age of 18.

Where can I get one?

You can buy a stocks-and-shares Isa direct from a fund management company, via a broker or fund platform or at a bank branch if the bank offers a stocks-and-shares product. Read on for our sections on how to buy shares and funds.

What should I use my Isa for?

Like any investment, you should analyse your risk and return and make a call on what you invest in and for how long. People generally invest in a stocks-and-shares Isa in order to generate a better return than is available from a cash savings account. You can invest in most types of investment including shares listed on recognised global stock exchanges, UK and European gilts, corporate bonds, investment trusts and funds. This makes them ideal for longer-term savings goals, such as boosting your retirement income.

Funds

Instead of buying assets – such as equities – directly, investors can pool their cash with others by investing in a collective fund. They invest across a wide range of companies, sectors, countries and even other funds. Collective funds allow investors to diversify their assets at the same time as accessing the experience of a professional fund manager. Investors can invest lump sums of as little as £1,000 or set up regular savings plans starting at £50 a month.

Collective funds are sometimes grouped into geographical areas such as the UK, Europe, the US or Far East, and can be further categorised by their investment strategy such as 'growth' or 'income'. There are thousands of funds split into many different sectors.

Because they are themselves diversified, most advisers recommend beginner investors start off by using collective funds rather than investing in single company shares directly, because they provide more diversification. They also get access to a professional fund manager who buys and sells the stocks within his or her fund.

It's worth noting that, while investment funds and investment trusts (see page 16) are actively managed products, run by a fund manager who hand-picks stocks and has some direction over the performance of the fund, you can also buy 'passive' funds, often called index-trackers. These vehicles simply track an index such as the FTSE 250 and are usually cheaper than funds or trusts because there is no active manager to pay for.

When indices rise, so too will your tracker fund, but an actively-managed fund may not – it depends on the expertise of the manager in picking the right stocks, even in a rising market. Similarly, if indices fall, so too will your tracker fund, but in this scenario an active fund has a chance of performing well – if the manager has picked stocks that outperform in a falling market. However, you will pay for such expertise and the majority of active funds do not perform better than the market average.

When you buy a collective investment, you'll usually pay an initial fee as well as an annual management charge (AMC). However, in reality, most people avoid the initial charge by not buying direct from the fund manager. Discount brokers and fund platforms typically rebate commissions to investors, reducing the initial charge to zero.

Many investors prefer to look at the ongoing charge on a fund, also known as the 'total expense ratio' (TER), as it offers a single snapshot of how much you are paying for a fund and makes it easy to see the impact of charges on returns.

The most common types of collective investment are unit trusts (sometimes known simply as 'funds') and investment companies (also known as 'investment trusts').

Unit trusts/funds

A unit trust is an investment fund shared by lots of different investors. The fund is divided into segments called 'units', which investors buy to own a stake in the fund. The price of each unit is based on the value of the assets owned by the fund.

Unit trusts are open-ended, meaning they get bigger as more people invest and smaller as investors withdraw their money. If a large number of investors wish to sell up at the same time, the unit trust manager may have to sell some of its assets in order to provide the money to satisfy these 'redemptions'.

Investors can buy and sell units through the fund manager or via a discount broker or fund platform. There are usually two different prices, making a unit trust a 'dual priced fund'. The two prices are:

- the offer price – the price you pay to buy units

- the bid price – the price you get for selling units.

The difference between the buying and selling price is known as the 'bid-offer spread' and it includes any initial charge and reflects the difference between the buying and selling prices of the underlying investments plus any costs involved in buying or selling them. The spread usually means that when investments are bought or sold as a result of other investors joining or leaving the fund, your investment is protected from these transaction costs.

Like most investments, there are charges that investors have to pay to cover the expenses of managing funds. These can vary considerably.

You might also come across open-ended investment companies (OEICs). These work in the same way as unit trusts but there are a couple of differences:

- OEICs package their investments into shares, not units

- OEIC units have a single price – there is no bid/offer spread.

Fund management groups began converting their unit trusts into OEICs in the early 2000s to bring them closer to the collective investment funds that are available in most EU countries – making it easier to market their UK funds across Europe. But, charging issues aside, OEICs and unit trusts are broadly similar from the investor's point of view: both are collective funds that seek to generate returns from investing in a broad range of assets.

The active versus passive debate

All investors need to understand the difference between actively managed funds and passive funds, often known as index trackers.

An active fund employs a manager to scour the investment universe to choose the assets he or she believes will most likely produce a decent return. Managers usually have whole teams of analysts, researchers and traders helping them to find these corporate gems. The aim is for this expertise to result in an active fund performing far better than the market they are focused on; such as a region like Asia, or a sector such as property or technology.

Passive funds are different. They avoid the whole concept of research and analysis and simply mimic a widely followed index. The goal is to hold every stock in an index such as the FTSE All Share or FTSE

100, with no attempt to outperform it. As a result, much of their trading is carried out automatically by computers.

So active funds aim to perform better than the market, while passive funds can never perform better than the market or index they track. For this reason, it is believed that active funds are particularly well-placed to perform well in a falling market: passive funds can only ever go down in a falling market, whereas a good manager will limit any damage and could even post a positive return.

But to complicate matters, in any given time period a large number of actively managed funds will fail to perform particularly well, making the search for a proven, star fund manager all-important. Fans of passive funds believe there is no point trying to find an active manager as none are skilled enough to deliver returns from such a complex beast as the stock market.

That said, passive funds can deviate from the indices they are supposed to track (known as tracking error), and no passive fund will exactly replicate the index it follows. So while investors may pay as little as 0.15% a year in fees for a tracker/passive fund, they must accept a different set of risks than those taken on by investors in actively managed funds.

When it comes to fees, active funds have that team of expensive managers and researchers to pay for, so they tend to be far more expensive than passive funds. But within the actively managed universe alone there is an incredibly diverse number of funds, all with different charges.

The highest charging funds tend to be 'funds of funds', which are funds that invest mainly in other funds, rather than individual assets such as equities or bonds.

A fund of funds will impose an extra layer of charges because investors are paying more than one lot of investment management fees.

While there is no right or wrong answer in the active versus passive debate, critics of actively managed funds argue that, because the majority underperform the index or benchmark that they seek to outperform, their higher fees are rarely justified.

But many active funds do deliver impressive returns. Investors' preferences will depend on their objectives and risk appetite, so putting a foot in both camps is sensible.

Investment trusts

Investment trusts are similar to unit trusts and OEICs in that they invest in shares, bonds or property and provide the opportunity for investors to spread risk. However, when you invest in an investment trust, you are buying shares in a company, not units in a fund. Investment trust shares are quoted on the stock market and you take a stake in an investment trust by buying its shares.

Investment trusts are 'closed-ended' funds because there are a set number of shares and this number does not change regardless of the number of investors.

Investment trusts are considered a slightly higher risk than unit trusts and OEICs because they are allowed to borrow money to invest – this is called 'gearing'. An investment trust that is geared is a higher-risk investment than one that is not geared because the manager has borrowed that extra cash with which to invest. Gearing can increase returns if the manager makes the correct investment call but it can amplify losses if the manager's purchases fall in value: the underlying assets will fall in value and the manager still owes the money borrowed.

However, while gearing can make investment trusts higher risk, a manager who is highly geared is likely to have a strong conviction that what they are investing in is a good prospect – or they wouldn't take on that additional risk.

The value of the assets held by an investment trust may be different from the actual share price, which means their shares can trade at a discount or a premium to the value of the underlying assets. This exaggerates the pattern of share-price performance – both upwards and downwards when compared to returns from unit trusts.

How to buy shares

You can purchase shares via a stockbroker. You'll have to open an account first, which is usually free.

Stockbrokers

You can use a discretionary broker, who will help run your portfolio for you, making buying and selling suggestions too, but these usually require a minimum investment level of £25,000 to £50,000.

Alternatively, you can choose an execution-only broker, which simply means one who will buy or sell whenever you tell them to, without offering any advice. Even if you do not require advice, most online brokers offer a wealth of company research and analysis on their sites, which execution-only investors can take advantage of, but you'll have to use your own judgement when researching this material.

You can trade via the telephone but most people trade online these days – it's quick and easy. Execution-only dealing can cost as little as £7 a trade (often called 'commission'), though some brokers' rates fall the more frequently you trade. Some charge an administration fee and an annual management fee if you have a lot of cash invested, plus you'll also have to pay government stamp duty on any trade of more than £1,000 (currently 0.5% rounded up to the nearest £5).

Here's a list of the major brokers and what they charge (at the time of writing) for single trades:

Barclays Stockbrokers

Online: 1-9 trades per month, £11.95; 10-19 trades per month, £8.95; 20-plus trades per month, £5.95

Hargreaves Lansdown

From £5.95 to £11.95 per trade, depending on the number of trades in the previous month. Phone and postal dealing: 1% (£20 minimum, £50 maximum)

Interactive Investor

£10 per trade, or £1.50 per trade in a regular investment plan, plus quarterly account fee of £20 (which covers your first two trades per quarter)

Selftrade

Online: £12.50 per trade; £6 each after 100 trades in a quarter. Phone: £17.50 per trade below £2,500; £40 per trade between £2,500 and £100,000

TD Direct Investing

Online: £12.50 per trade, £8.95 if ten or more trades in the previous three months, or £5.95 if 20 or more trades in the previous three months. Regular investment account: £1.50 per trade

The Share Centre

Sharedealing: 1% (£7.50 minimum). Trader option: £7.50 per trade.

How to buy funds/trusts

The costs involved in buying funds and trusts can vary massively, and higher fees can easily eat away at future returns. To ensure value for money, you should compare charges on different products.

When you buy a fund, you pay a couple of different fees. First up is the initial fee, which can be up to 5.5% of the sum you are investing. This means that if you invest £20,000 in a fund with an initial charge of 5%, you will be investing only £19,000 – the other £1,000 will be eaten up in charges.

You then pay an annual management fee, which can be a further 1.5%. Higher-risk funds tend to have higher annual management fees, while tracker (passive) funds tend to have lower charges.

Some investment vehicles also charge exit fees, while a fund in which the manager is constantly selling and buying shares or other assets will see some of your cash further eroded by the manager's own trading fees.

Some actively managed funds may also charge a performance fee on top of all of that – making it increasingly difficult for investors to generate a decent net return after fees.

Investors should pay particular attention to a fund's total annual cost, known as the 'total expense ratio' (TER) or 'ongoing charge' (OCF), as this takes into account almost all the above fees to give you a true reflection of the cost of the fund. The TER divides the total costs of your fund (management fees, trading charges, etc.) by its assets to produce a single percentage. If your fund generates a return in one year of 8% but has a TER of 3%, it means the gain is actually 5% after fees.

There are three different ways investors can buy funds: direct from the fund manager; via a financial adviser; or via a fund platform or execution-only broker. The latter ways of investing are generally cheaper than buying direct because many fund platforms, brokers (and even advisers) negotiate price reductions with fund management groups so that when you buy through them the annual management charge (AMC) applied by the fund management group will be lower.

However, you will pay platform charges, which vary considerably. Execution-only brokers that operate platforms can charge around 0.4% per annum (sometimes more), while platforms run by advisers tend to charge less, at around 0.25% to 0.3% a year. You might also pay additional costs such as exit penalties if you wish to move your investments to an alternative platform or adviser.

It's worth noting that since the introduction of the Retail Distribution Review (RDR) in January 2013, financial advisers have no longer been able to take commission on any investments they sell. As a result, commission and platform charges have been stripped away from fund charges when sold by an adviser (though fund platforms had until April 2015 to be fully switched to these 'clean' shares only).

So platforms are now offering clean or 'unbundled' share classes, which do not already have the commission bundled in. They should, in theory, be cheaper. But until the full switchover to clean-only share classes is complete, many funds have both clean and 'dirty' versions available to buy.

To further complicate matters, some platforms and advisers have negotiated price reductions with investment companies so that if you buy via them, the price of your units or shares will be lower still. These have become known as 'super clean' shares.

Lump sum versus regular investing

Beginner investors will usually either start off with a lump sum because they have inherited some money or had a windfall, or they will dip a toe in the water by making small, regular monthly investments.

Regular savings are a good way to smooth out the volatility of the stock market, reducing risk and boosting returns over the long term. But a lump sum means all your cash is fully invested from the get-go and can lead to fantastic returns over the long term.

With regular saving, your monthly cash will buy you a larger number of shares or fund units in months when the market falls and prices drop. But many people sometimes stop making payments when markets fall – even though this is exactly when they should continue investing as they are getting more for their money. So if you do decide to invest regularly, try not to get the jitters the first time you have a bad month – and if in doubt, speak to a financial adviser.

Getting financial advice

Many people choose to use the services of a qualified financial adviser because they don't know enough about investing. It makes sense – you wouldn't try to build a house without using a builder, and you wouldn't try to diagnose a friend's illness yourself.

In the same way, an independent financial adviser (IFA) can be invaluable in making sure your money is working as hard as it can for you. Some won't even charge for an initial consultation, as it's a good chance for them to find out about you – and for you to ask them what their charges are.

Following the RDR, financial advisers can no longer take commission from product providers and clients must now pay an upfront fee.

Fees will vary from adviser to adviser but you can expect to pay about £150 an hour for good advice. However, according to professional adviser website Unbiased, an IFA who helps you to review your investments or set up your pension may be happy to do this for a fixed charge for the whole job and there's no harm in seeing if there is any room for negotiation or the ability to pay in instalments.

Breakdown of adviser fees

- Advice fee: the cost that a professional adviser charges for providing their services. This is subject to VAT at the standard rate.

- Fixed fee: some advisers may be prepared to undertake a specific task for a fixed fee, such as setting up a pension policy. Make sure you ask them precisely what is and isn't included.

- Hourly rate: where the client pays for each hour (or part hour) of the adviser's time. You should be given an estimate of how long the work will take and, therefore, how much you might expect to pay. Ask if any of the work can be carried out by a more junior colleague and then signed off by someone senior to save you money.

- Percentage of assets: often used by wealth managers who manage a portfolio of assets and investments for their clients. They take payment for their services based on a percentage of the value of the total portfolio.

- Retainer: in financial advice, this is similar to 'percentage of assets' where the adviser takes payment based on an agreed percentage of the value of the assets or by working out a time/cost basis for regular management of your financial affairs.

- Commission: where the adviser takes payment for their services as commission from the company you buy your product from. After the Retail Distribution Review, financial advisers are no longer able to take commission on products that can be broadly described as investments – which include pensions, equity release, life policies, investments in unit trusts and other kinds of investment. There are some financial 'products' (such as insurance or mortgages) advisers are still allowed to be paid for by commission – ask your adviser.

Pensions and retirement

When you've started your first job and life is full of after-work parties, weekend city breaks and summer holidays in glamorous locations, it's easy to push thoughts of retirement to the back of your mind.

But the sooner you can begin to save for retirement, the more money you could make and the more likely it is that you will be able to enjoy a comfortable lifestyle in your later years.

Unfortunately, most of us delay contributing to a pension and when we finally begin, we often fail to save enough to generate a decent income in retirement. This means many people have to rely on the State Pension, worth not much more than £600 a month.

An added problem is that we are living longer, meaning we require more money to fund our retirement years. Actuaries say that one in four children born today will live to be 100, compared to just one in ten 50 years ago.

With this in mind, it's crucial that you begin thinking about pensions from an early age and, if you can, begin making provisions over and above the State Pension. Here's our guide to how pensions work and how you can make your money work hardest for you. But remember, pension payments are classed as income and are subject to income tax (should you earn enough in total for them to be taxable).

State Pension

The basic State Pension is a weekly payment from the government that you get when you reach State Pension age. How much you currently receive depends on your age, work history, marital status and where in the world you live.

Crucially, the pension you receive depends on how many years' worth of National Insurance (NI) contributions you have made. You need 30 years' contributions or credits (known as 'qualifying years') to get the full basic State Pension. If you have fewer than this, your State Pension will simply be less. Bear in mind, however, that this is rising to 35 years' worth of NI contributions from 2016.

How much is it worth?

For those reaching state retirement age before April 2017, the basic State Pension is worth up to £115.95 a week (in the tax year 2015/16).

The value of the basic State Pension rises every April, increasing by the higher of inflation, average earnings or a minimum of 2.5% (known as the 'triple lock'). However, from April 2016, the current State Pension arrangements will be replaced by a single state scheme, which the government has touted at a 'flat rate' of no less than £148.40 a week. Some will receive more and some less. For example, as we've said, to qualify for the full amount, you'll need to have made NI contributions for 35 years instead of the current 30. However, if you don't have the full 35 years' worth, NI credits are available to people who have been in receipt of certain unemployment or sickness benefits as well as those that have taken time out of work to raise children or care for somebody who is sick or disabled. If you still don't have enough credits, you can make top-up contributions (see page 28).

You become eligible to receive the basic State Pension upon reaching state retirement age, which used to be 60 for a woman and 65 for a man. However, this changed from 6 April 2010 and the retirement age for men and women is gradually being made the same.

For women, these rises are steep, rising to age 65 by 2018. Then both sexes will see their state retirement age rise in stages: to 66 by 2020 and to 68 by 2046. The pension age will, in future, be linked to longevity and reviewed every five years. Actuaries predict this could mean that today's 33-year-olds will have a State Pension age of 73.

How do I make NI contributions?

When you're working, you automatically pay National Insurance via PAYE if you're employed and earning more than £8,060 (£155 a week). If you're self-employed, you can also make NI contributions. You will start building up qualifying years at the start of the tax year in which you turn 16, and you'll finish at the end of the tax year before you reach State Pension age.

If you're not working, the government will, in some circumstances, give you NI credits that count towards the basic State Pension, so you don't lose out. Since April 2010, you receive NI credits if you care for a child under the age of 12; for someone sick or disabled; if you are a registered foster carer; or you get Carer's Allowance.

If you haven't made enough NI contributions, you can choose to make up the shortfall in order to qualify for the full State Pension by making top-up contributions. To check how much you may be entitled to, you can get a State Pension forecast at **gov.uk/state-pension**.

Deferring your State Pension

You can earn extra State Pension if you defer taking it for at least five weeks. In return, the government will increase it by 1% for every five weeks you defer claiming it, equivalent to 10.4% over a whole year. Alternatively, you can choose to get a one-off lump sum payment if you put off claiming your State Pension for at least 12 months in a row. This will include interest of 2% above the Bank of England base rate.

According to consumer rights group Which?, during the 2014/15 tax year those deferring for one year got an extra £595 – increasing their weekly State Pension from £113.10 to £124.54 in today's money. After three years' deferral, they'd get an extra £1,787 a year, or a weekly pension starting at £147.47. After five years, the deferred pension would increase by an annual £2,978 or a weekly income of £170.40.

That said, if you're eligible for the State Pension at age 65 and defer for five years, you won't earn back the pension you sacrificed until you reach 79.

Deferring could work well for those who plan to work on after state retirement age anyway but the benefits will be less generous for those who reach this age after 2016.

However, the benefits of deferral are being reduced. From April 2016, the deferral rate will fall to 5.8% and the option to take a lump sum will be removed. This means you'll need to live much longer to make deferring worthwhile.

Pension Credit

Pension Credit is designed to top up the finances of pensioners whose income falls below minimum levels, offering them an extra, albeit thin, safety net.

The benefit is made up of two parts: the Guarantee Credit, which ensures your income meets a certain threshold; and the Savings Credit, which rewards pensioners who have saved for retirement and have a small amount of income from a private pension.

To be eligible for Pension Credit, you need to meet certain age and income requirements.

The qualifying age for Guarantee Credit is gradually increasing to 66, in line with the increase in State Pension age for women to 65 and the further increase to 66 for men and women. To check the exact age at which you can begin receiving State Pension (and thus Guarantee Credit), visit **gov.uk**.

In order to qualify for Guarantee Credit, your weekly income needs to be below £151.20 (2015/16) if you are single, rising to £230.85 for couples. Unlike benefits that pay a fixed amount (like Child Benefit or Jobseeker's Allowance), Guarantee Credit literally tops up your income to a minimum level, so how much you receive will depend on your income.

When you apply, the following will be used to work out your income: State Pension (basic and additional); other pensions; most social security benefits – for example, Carer's Allowance; savings and investments over £10,000 – for these, £1 is counted for every £500 or part-£500; and earnings.

The following isn't included when your income is worked out: Attendance Allowance; Christmas Bonus; Disability Living Allowance; Personal Independence Payment; Housing Benefit; and Council Tax Reduction.

To qualify for the extra Savings Credit, you or your partner must be 65 or over. You're treated as a couple if you live with your husband, wife or partner; you don't have to be married or in a civil partnership.

Savings Credit aims to reduce the detrimental impact of any private pension income on the overall amount you are able to claim. It pays 60% of any income you receive over and above the basic State Pension weekly payment (currently £115.95 a week) up to a maximum of £14.82 a week for singles and £17.43 for couples.

However, once your income goes above the Guarantee Credit threshold, you start to lose Savings Credit at a rate of 40p for every £1. That said, some people – including carers, those with severe disabilities or specific housing costs – may get more.

It can be a difficult calculation, so check out **gov.uk**'s Pension Credit calculator to get an idea of how much you could be entitled to.

If you claim Pension Credit, you could also benefit from the Cold Weather Payment. This pays £25 if the temperature falls below 0°C for seven consecutive days between 1 November and 1 March. If there are four such periods between these dates, you'll receive £100 in total. If you are eligible, it should automatically be paid into the account into which you receive the rest of your benefits within 14 days of the cold weather.

A £10 Christmas Bonus is also paid to all Pension Credit claimants. Unlike some benefits, such as Incapacity Benefit, Jobseeker's Allowance and the Carer's Allowance, Pension Credit payments are not subject to tax.

How you can claim Pension Credit

To claim, you'll need your National Insurance number, bank account details and information about your income, savings and investments. You can apply for Pension Credit four months before you become eligible. Unfortunately, claims can be backdated by only three months so it's important to put in a claim as soon as possible.

In 2016, when the new flat-rate State Pension is introduced, Pension Credit will continue to be paid to existing claimants. However, it is expected that fewer pensioners will need to claim in the future. A means-tested top-up will remain to ensure there is still a safety net in place for the poorest pensioners.

Workplace pensions

As we've established, a State Pension of less than £150 a week will not be enough for most people to live on comfortably in retirement – especially if you still have mortgage or rent payments to make. So it's a good idea to make alternative provisions for your future. The most common way of doing so is via a pension fund and many employed people will be offered the chance to invest in one via their workplace pension scheme.

A workplace scheme allows you to save for your retirement via contributions deducted direct from your wages. Many employers also make contributions on your behalf.

In 2012, the government introduced auto-enrolment, which requires employers to automatically enrol most of their workforce into a pension scheme. Unless employees opt out, usually both the employer and the employee must pay contributions into the scheme (although it is possible for the employer to pay all the contributions).

Companies with 120,000 or more employees joined the auto-enrolment scheme upon its launch in October 2012. Smaller companies will be required to join in stages, with the smallest ones (fewer than 30 employees) joining from 1 January 2016. However, you'll be automatically enrolled only if you're 22 or older and earn more than £10,000 a year before tax.

Whether you are automatically enrolled or not, there are different types of workplace pension scheme, offering different benefits. If your employer does not offer an occupational scheme, it will offer you access to a group personal pension or a stakeholder pension.

Occupational schemes

Employers set up occupational pension schemes to provide pensions for their employees. They come in two forms: final salary schemes and money purchase schemes (often referred to, respectively, as 'defined benefit' and 'defined contribution' schemes).

Final salary schemes are now scarce to non-existent in the private sector because they became too expensive and risky for employers to run. However, they are still prevalent in the public sector. Your pension is calculated based on your final salary at retirement and the number of years you have contributed to the scheme; it pays a fraction (say 1/60th) of your final salary for every year you have been a member of the scheme. This means that, unlike defined contribution schemes, your pension is not dependent on the performance of the stock market and/or other investments.

Money purchase schemes are called 'defined contribution' schemes because only the amount you put into the scheme is guaranteed. Once you (and possibly your employer) have paid the money in, it is invested in the stock market and other investments via a pension fund. As these investments increase in value, so does the pension fund to provide you with a decent retirement pot. So your pension upon retirement is based on how much you paid in and how your investments performed.

You'll usually pay a percentage of your wages into the scheme and your employer might also match this or pay in a certain amount (though not all employers offer this perk). You will receive tax relief on your contributions as well, making them a highly attractive means of saving.

It's generally considered to be a good idea to join a scheme to which your employer makes contributions; if your employer doesn't yet through auto-enrolment, it might be worth looking at an alternative private pension provider as the pension funds offered by your employer may be inferior to others on the market.

Because a money purchase scheme does not guarantee a set pension when you retire, you must decide what to do with your pot of money. Under the new pension freedoms, savers essentially have three key options – cash in your pension and take the money; leave it invested and use it to generate an income; or buy an annuity. And you aren't limited to choosing just one option: you can mix and match to provide the right solution for you. You could, for example, take some cash to pay for any retirement trips, take an annuity to cover your regular bills and leave some invested for your long-term financial security.

Sadly, there is no one-size-fits-all plan; what makes most sense for you will depend on a whole host of factors including your age, state of health, the size of your pension, your attitude to risk, your desire to leave an inheritance and your needs for flexibility and or security. More on this below.

Occupational pension schemes often offer additional benefits over and above the pension itself, such as: life insurance, which pays out a lump sum or pension to your dependants if you die while still employed (this is usually four times your salary); a pension if you have to retire early because of ill health; and even a pension for your wife, husband, civil partner or other dependant when you die. These are usually referred to as 'death-in-service benefits'.

If your employer doesn't operate its own pension scheme, it may offer you access to a group personal pension or a stakeholder pension. Your employer will choose the pension provider but you will have an individual contract with that provider. It works in a similar way to a workplace defined contribution scheme, in that you pay contributions into the pension fund direct from your wages and that cash is invested, via the pension fund, in the stock market.

Personal pensions

If you do not wish to invest in your workplace pension, you are able to choose a pension off the shelf from the open market and do the whole thing yourself. Personal pensions work in the same way as any other pension that invests in the stock market. They are most suited to those who are working but are ineligible for auto-enrolment into their employer's pension scheme, the self-employed and those not working at all.

Stakeholder pensions

A stakeholder pension is a personal pension that must adhere to a number of rules designed to make them cheap and easy for consumers to understand. These rules are:

- the pension provider is not allowed to charge more than 1% of the value of your fund each year for administering the pension

- minimum contributions are £20, although you should make more than this if you can

- it's up to you how and when you make payments into your fund – you can't be forced to pay in regularly

- there are no penalties for missing or stopping payments

- you can switch your fund to another stakeholder scheme or other pension at any time without penalty.

Self-invested personal pensions (Sipps)

These allow you to choose and manage your own investments. They allow individuals to invest in a broad range of assets, some of which are high risk. They also have higher charges than personal and stakeholder pensions, reflecting the risks involved in self-management, although these fees have fallen in recent years.

This is why Sipps have historically been operated by wealthier people and sophisticated investors, who either run the Sipp themselves or pay a wealth manager to do it for them. That is changing as they become cheaper and they are increasingly a viable option for anyone who wishes to take control of their retirement savings.

Contributions

The government encourages you to save for your retirement by giving you tax relief on pension contributions, which reduces your tax bill or increases your pension fund. You can save as much as you like in as many different pensions as you like, and receive tax relief on contributions of up to 100% of your earnings each year (though contributions above £40,000 a year may be taxed at 40%). Also, contributions are subject to a lifetime allowance of £1.25 million, falling to £1 million from April 2016.

With an occupational scheme, your employer takes the pension contributions from your pay before deducting tax (but not National Insurance contributions). This means you only pay tax on what's left. So whether you pay tax at the basic, higher or additional rate, you get the full relief straightaway.

With a personal pension, you pay income tax on your earnings before any pension contribution but the pension provider claims tax back from the government at the basic rate of 20%. In practice, this means that for every £80 you pay into your pension, you end up with £100 in your pension pot. If you pay tax at the higher rate, you can claim the difference through your tax return, or by telephoning or writing to HM Revenue & Customs (HMRC).

As an example, broker Hargreaves Lansdown says that if you contribute £8,000 into your pension, the government adds £2,000, to make a total investment of £10,000. Higher- and additional-rate taxpayers can then claim back even more via their tax return. It means that £10,000 in a pension could therefore effectively cost a higher-rate taxpayer as little as £6,000 and an additional-rate taxpayer just £5,500.

Choosing a pension

According to the government's own Money Advice Service, if you're an employee and you're not already contributing to a workplace scheme, your first step should be to find out what kind of pension scheme your employer offers.

If your employer makes contributions to your pension too, then joining the scheme will almost always make sense. After all, if you don't sign up, you're effectively turning down additional pay from your employer.

Make sure the charges are low, too. Pensions are more competitive than they used to be but they can still be expensive and this is why the government is proposing (at the time of writing) to cap pension fund charges at 0.75%. For now, stakeholder pensions have low charges, and so do many workplace schemes. Sipp fees have been falling too, making them increasingly competitive.

Watch out also for start-up fees when joining the scheme or separate charges on the contributions you make each year, although these don't apply to stakeholder pensions. The charges will all be set out in the 'Key Facts' document. The Money Advice Service adds that you should then shop around. Its own comparison tables for stakeholder and personal pensions can help you find the most appropriate pension for you.

Also consider how flexible the pension is. With some personal pensions, you're obliged to pay in a regular sum every month. That can be difficult if you're self-employed and your income varies, or if your bills vary from month to month. If this applies to you, go for a pension that allows you to pay in different amounts every month, and/or lump sums. All stakeholder pensions are flexible.

You'll also need to decide how the money you put in your pension scheme should be invested. You'll probably have a range of investment funds to choose from, and finding the best investment strategy depends on a wide range of factors, such as how close you are to your planned retirement date and your attitude to financial risk.

Get any advice you need. Saving for your retirement is crucial, but it involves some very important decisions along the way. You should be as informed as possible before making these decisions. You can do a lot of the research yourself but if you are in any doubt, seek independent financial advice.

When and how you should take your pension

Making money through investment to secure a comfortable lifestyle in retirement is one thing but deciding exactly how to maximise your income once you do finally stop working is just as tricky. The 2014 Budget relaxed a number of the restrictive rules governing how you can turn your pension into retirement income (more on this below).

Under HMRC rules, the earliest age at which you can normally start taking your pension is 55. If your pension starts earlier than this, it will be an unauthorised payment and both you and your scheme administrator will pay extra tax on the pension. There is an exception to this rule: if you're suffering from ill health.

You don't have to leave your job to start taking your pension. If your scheme rules allow it, you can continue working after you've started your pension. Moreover, you don't have to use all your pension pot to provide your pension at the same time. For example, if your scheme allows it, you could take part of your pension and continue working, and then when you leave your employer, you can take the rest.

To answer the question of when to take your pension, you need to ask yourself: will I have enough to live on comfortably in retirement? If you intend to rely on the State Pension to provide the lion's share of your pension income, the answer is almost certainly 'no'. Unfortunately, even if you have been contributing each year to a private pension scheme, you may still not have saved enough to generate enough income to live on in retirement.

If you plan to continue working, there is still time to recover the situation. Even if you are at the point of retiring, by making the right choices you can boost the income you receive for the rest of your life.

First, think about when you want to retire, what retirement income you would like and where that income will come from. Be realistic: is retiring at age 60 or earlier something that will realistically be possible? If not, you might need to delay your retirement.

You can find out how much pension you are likely to get and what difference investing more can make by putting your details into the government's Money Advice Service pension calculator, which can be found at **moneyadviceservice.org.uk**.

Upon retirement, most people purchase an annuity. Essentially, it's an insurance policy – in exchange for your pension fund, it pays you a guaranteed income for the rest of your life.

HMRC will allow you to take 25% as an immediate tax-free cash lump sum, while you can choose to annuitise the rest, keep it invested or even withdraw the lot (but you'll pay tax at your marginal rate if you opt for the latter).

HMRC cannot control how or what you choose to spend your money on – so, should you wish, you're free to buy that speedboat you always wanted. But prudence is just as important as you approach your retirement years as it was when you were diligently making pension contributions throughout your working life.

Annuities

An annuity can arguably be the most important thing you ever buy: currently it's a decision that can't be reversed. George Osborne has proposed that retirees should be able to sell their annuities if they wish, but even if this does get the green light, you won't get back the full value of your plan, so it's vital that you do your research before you take the plunge or seek the advice of an independent financial adviser. Here's an eight-point checklist.

1. **Find out what your pension provider will offer you:** Six months before you are due to retire, your pension provider is obliged to contact you, sending a retirement pack with a letter informing you of what income you can expect to receive if you use it to purchase an annuity. But you can contact your provider earlier than this if you are keen to work out what income you might expect in retirement.

    In the majority of cases, you will be able to get a better deal elsewhere. Indeed, in 2014 the regulator announced an investigation into annuities, claiming people were simply not shopping around enough before making their decision – and getting poor value annuities as a result. That said, if you bought a pension in the 1970s and 1980s that had a guaranteed annuity rate (GAR) attached, you'll probably get a decent rate as these stem from a time when interest rates were so much higher. Just be careful you retire at the right time, as the GAR may only apply if you retire on your scheme's selected retirement date – for example, your 65th birthday. Moreover, remember that while the income may be higher, you may not be able to include inflation-proofing or preserve an income for your dependants if you die before them.

2. **Shop around:** Once you know what your pension provider will offer you, use a comparison website to find out what rival

annuity providers will pay you in retirement. These websites also allow you to experiment with different options to show you what impact they will have on your overall income.

3. **Tell your provider about any health problems or vices:** Admitting you drink like a fish or smoke 40 a day could result in you getting a better annuity rate. To be eligible for an enhanced annuity – which pays higher rates to those who are expected to have a lower life expectancy – you don't have to be seriously ill. Lifestyle issues such as drinking, smoking or being overweight could get you an enhanced annuity because actuaries believe you may not live as long. The same applies with health complaints including diabetes, raised blood pressure or cholesterol. According to Hargreaves Lansdown, 56% of retirees would qualify for an enhanced annuity. For instance, a smoker with high blood pressure and cholesterol readings could get an enhanced income of up to 47%.

4. **Single or joint annuity?** A single annuity simply stops paying when you die but a joint one will carry on paying your spouse until he/she dies. You can choose for 100% of the income to be paid after your death, or a reduced proportion, such as two-thirds or half. Single-life annuities will pay the highest income but failure to purchase protection for a spouse could have disastrous consequences if you die first and your spouse does not have enough income to live on.

5. **Do you want a guaranteed payment?** An annuity without any guarantee will stop paying when the policyholder dies, meaning any surviving family members will get nothing. To prevent this, you can purchase a guarantee that will ensure your income is paid for a minimum period after you die. So if you purchased an annuity with a five-year guarantee but were to die after three years, the policy would continue to pay an income to your family for another two years. Most annuities are sold with a five-year guarantee.

6. **Do you want inflation protection?** You will also be asked if you want to receive an income that remains the same for the duration of the policy or an escalating one that increases with inflation. The level of income will be higher at the outset with the policy that pays the same income throughout, but the escalating option will

pay an increased income with time. You can opt for either fixed percentage increases – say 3% a year – or increases that are directly linked to the inflation measure, the Retail Prices Index (RPI).

However, inflation linking doesn't always pay. Research from MGM Advantage found that you might have to live a very long time before it pays off.

Taking the example of a £100,000 annuity over the typical 22-year retirement, it found that a level annuity paying £5,743 a year would pay out a total income of £126,346 but an RPI-linked plan paying £3,331 at outset rising to £6,197 in the final year would only pay out £101,718 in total. An escalating annuity rising at 3% a year would start out paying £3,929 rising to £7,309 in the 22nd year, paying out a total of £119,979.

MGM's research found that an investment-linked annuity might offer better protection against inflation. The same £100,000 pot would buy a starting income of £5,740, rising to £7,895 in year 22 and paying out a total of £145,655. However, because these plans remain invested and there is the potential for your income and capital to fall, they are suited only to wealthier investors with a higher tolerance of risk.

7. **Check out the alternatives:** Rule changes mean that you no longer have to purchase an annuity. For example, you can leave your money invested and go for income drawdown – this gives you the ability to retain control of your money and you can vary the income you receive as and when your circumstances change. Unlike annuities, you will have a choice of death benefits – your dependants could convert the fund into an annuity, carry on taking an income, or take a lump sum. Alternatively, you could consider flexible or short-term annuities.

8. **Take advice:** If you're in any way unsure, or don't think an annuity is appropriate for you, it is well worth paying for independent financial advice. This might seem expensive but it may not cost you any more than buying through a discount broker that will be taking a slice of your income in commission. You may also get a higher income or an arrangement that is better suited to you.

Taking a 25% lump sum

HMRC allows you to take a whopping 25% of your pension as a tax-free lump sum. You can actually withdraw as much as you like, whenever you like, but only the first 25% will be tax-free; the remainder will be charged at your marginal rate of tax (the highest rate of income tax you pay).

The 25% lump sum can be withdrawn from your pension fund whether you have invested in a defined-contribution (or money purchase) scheme, or a defined-benefit (final salary or career average) scheme. However, the benefit varies considerably depending on what type of scheme you are invested in, and other factors such as the size of your fund and your state of health will also affect your final decision.

Taking your tax-free cash from a money purchase scheme is a fairly straightforward decision, even if you want to maximise the income you can generate from your savings. Provided that you use tax-efficient wrappers such as Isas, it can continue growing and generating an income tax-free. But if instead you were to use this money to buy an annuity, the resulting income would be assessable for tax.

The income you generate by investing your tax-free lump sum might not be as high as that produced by an annuity. A £100,000 pension fund would buy a 65-year-old a level-term annuity of £5,800 a year, according to Hargreaves Lansdown, but the income generated by a £75,000 annuity combined with a £25,000 investment in an equity income multi-manager fund yielding 3.95% would produce a total of about £5,350.

There are still advantages to this route: the investor has access to the £25,000, and there is potential for the investment and the income it generates to grow. However, such funds can fall in value too, whereas an annuity gives you certainty and is paid for life, something that shouldn't be underestimated – even if annuity rates have been poor in recent years.

Deciding whether to take tax-free cash from a defined benefit pension is much more complicated, as the impact on retirement income is potentially much greater, dependent as they are on 'commutation factors' – the figures used to work out how much pension income you have to give up for a certain amount of tax-free cash. Hargreaves Lansdown says that for a defined benefit scheme from which the saver has a £10,000 annual income (before taking tax-free cash), the amount they could withdraw as cash would typically be £46,000, leaving them with a residual income of £6,900 a year.

The important thing to remember is that the income from a final salary scheme is increased in line with inflation each year, which is a valuable benefit.

Income drawdown

Many modern defined contribution schemes have been designed to enable you to take your pension in stages through income drawdown, where you leave the money invested and withdraw an income rather than buying an annuity. The benefit of this is that you retain ownership and control of your money and the income you take from it.

The amount of income you can draw down is no longer capped, as it was before the start of the 2015/16 tax year (when retirees could only draw down 120% of the income they would have been able to get with a single-life conventional annuity, rising to 150% between 27 March 2014 and 5 April 2015).

If you are planning a phased retirement, gradually decreasing the amount you work, then taking income drawdown offers considerable tax advantages, both during your lifetime and after. But it's worth noting again that your invested pension is subject to the whims of the stock market and could fall in value.

The reality of equity release

To top up income in retirement, tens of thousands of over-55s turn to equity release every year to unlock capital built up in their homes.

Equity release is an arrangement with an insurance company that allows you to take some of the value of your property as cash while still being able to live in it.

You borrow a lump sum – the size of which depends on your age and the value of your property – and compound interest starts to build up on the loan.

Unlike most other loans where monthly repayments start immediately, an equity release loan only has to be settled on death or on moving into a care home.

Equity release is growing in popularity, with the Equity Release Council reporting the industry is on course to see 20,000 new customers having released cash in 2014 – up from just under 19,000 in 2013. The council's latest figures at the time of writing revealed the average amount of money freed up per person during July to September 2014 was £67,467.

According to research by Just Retirement, most people use the money to clear their mortgage, pay for home improvements and clear debt.

So how exactly does it work?

The most commonly bought equity release product is a lifetime mortgage. The customer gets a lump sum or smaller regular amounts of money while retaining ownership of their home. Interest builds up on the loan to be repaid by their estate upon death or on moving into long-term care. For couples, repayment will not be due until the last remaining person living in the home either dies or moves into care.

However, there are significant costs to be aware of. The interest rate charged will be higher than on a standard mortgage, given the long-term nature of the product. For example, at the time of writing lifetime mortgage lender LV= charged 6.19% on its lifetime mortgage for 60- to 80-year-olds. The interest rolls up each month, meaning that each year you'll be racking up interest on a bigger debt. As a result, the longer the loan lasts the more costly it becomes.

For example, take a £50,000 loan with a rate of 6.19%. According to LV= after one year that debt plus interest would be £53,095, over ten years it would become £91,160 and after 20 years that £50,000 loan will have more than tripled in size to become a £166,204 debt (see box below).

There are also charges to factor in. LV= says these can be around £2,500 for an equity release arrangement fee, which includes a valuation fee of £222, an application fee of £595, a solicitor's fee of £500 and an financial adviser fee of £1,000. But you'll never owe more than the value of your home.

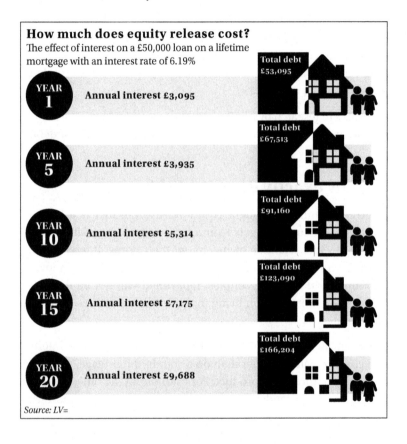

How much does equity release cost?
The effect of interest on a £50,000 loan on a lifetime mortgage with an interest rate of 6.19%

YEAR **1** — Annual interest £3,095 — Total debt £53,095

YEAR **5** — Annual interest £3,935 — Total debt £67,513

YEAR **10** — Annual interest £5,314 — Total debt £91,160

YEAR **15** — Annual interest £7,175 — Total debt £123,090

YEAR **20** — Annual interest £9,688 — Total debt £166,204

Source: LV=

Starting a business

Starting a business is a great way to change your lifestyle. You could ditch the commute and find a much better work-life balance by being your own boss. But working for yourself requires you to put on your financial head so that you make money, not waste money.

Here's a list of tips to help you get started:

1. **Do your homework.** Thorough market research is vital. No business can make money without people willing to pay for your product or service. So before you spend a penny on your business idea, you must make sure you know who your customers will be.

   You also need to work out who your competition is. Are there other firms or individuals already doing what you're planning to do? If so, ask yourself if there is enough business for both/ all of you. Why would customers come to you instead? Can you compete on price? What would make your version better?

2. **Work out how much money you will need to start and run your business.** It doesn't matter what you're selling – cakes you've baked or your bookkeeping skills – every business encounters overheads that need paying for such as rent, electricity bills and equipment costs. So write yourself a list of all the likely outgoings you'll come across before you receive payment from your first customer.

3. **Prepare a business plan.** This will be key in securing any funding, such as a business loan from the bank. A robust plan will demonstrate your knowledge and understanding of your product or service and the market it operates in. It will include detailed information on costs, debts, who the customer is, and how much money is expected to be made – and when. It should also explain how additional funding or investment could be used to grow the business.

4. **Get yourself a business bank account.** Running your business finances from one dedicated account makes it much easier to keep an eye on your costs and your profit. And having an

overdraft can be very useful when you're starting out and you have bills to pay before your first invoice has been paid.

5. **Find out if any start-up funding is available.** When savings and loans from friends and family dry up, entrepreneurs must turn elsewhere for investment. Loans are available from banks and, depending what area of business you are in, you could also get help from your local authority or from the government. You could look for funding from investors, too, by way of venture capitalism and crowdfunding (for more on crowdfunding see page 97).

6. **Make sure your insurance is adequate.** If you will be working from home, make sure your contents insurance covers any stock you might have.

For further information on starting up a business, visit the following websites:

- **startupbritain.co.uk**
- **ideastap.com**
- **startuploans.co.uk**
- **www.fsb.org.uk**
- **smallbusiness.co.uk**
- **gov.uk/starting-up-a-business**

Buying and selling property

Buying a property will probably be the most expensive purchase you ever make but there is serious money to be made if you tread carefully. But whether it's your first or your fifth property purchase, it can be a stressful experience.

Buyers all too often get caught up in the emotion of setting up a home. But instead of falling in love with a house, making an offer on it and then trying to arrange your finances, you will put yourself in a far stronger position if you get your finances in place before you start house-hunting.

If you need a mortgage to buy your home, you should work out exactly how much you can put down as a deposit and afford to borrow, as well as organise all the supporting documentation your mortgage provider and solicitor will require from you.

Buying your first home can be a daunting experience but remember that being a first-time buyer automatically puts you in a stronger position. Take confidence in the fact that those with property to sell appreciate first-time buyers because they are able to proceed quickly: they don't have to sell anything before they can commit to buy.

However, while first-timers might be able to offer sellers quick sales, buying a home involves conveyancing, a complicated legal process, so don't expect the purchase to happen overnight. The experts say it currently takes around eight weeks for first-timers to complete on a home purchase.

Whether you're a first-timer or not, here's a run-through of everything you're likely to encounter when you buy a new home and some tips to make the process as straightforward and speedy as possible.

What you can borrow

Before you start viewing properties, find out exactly what you can afford to spend on your home. Don't make the mistake of thinking the lump sum you'll have to put down for the deposit is all you'll need to pay upfront. You'll also have to pay for stamp duty (more on this later), mortgage fees, legal fees, surveys and valuations. Then there are the actual moving costs and the costs of furnishing the property.

How much a mortgage provider will lend you depends mostly on how much you earn. On average, providers will lend between three and four times your salary. So someone on a salary of £30,000 can expect to borrow anything from around £90,000 to £120,000.

If you are taking out a mortgage jointly with someone else, some lenders will offer a choice of two options:

1. **Adding the lower income to the original multiple** – so if the main breadwinner earns £30,000 and the other person earns £25,000, a lender might offer four times the first income plus the second income (4 x £30,000 + £25,000 = £145,000).

2. **Adding the two incomes together and then offering a lower multiple** – so instead of lending four times the biggest salary, it may offer three times the combined earnings (£30,000 + £25,000 = £55,000; then £55,000 x 3 = £165,000).

There are lots of other factors that determine exactly how much you can borrow, the most important of which is the amount of money you wish to borrow as a proportion of the property value, referred to as the loan-to-value (or LTV) ratio.

For example, a borrower wishing to buy a £200,000 home who has enough saved to put down a £20,000 deposit needs to borrow 90% of the property's value – so that person needs a 90% LTV mortgage. This is a typical LTV for a first-time buyer but the ratio can be as high as 95%.

In general, the smaller the deposit you put down and the higher the LTV ratio you need, the higher the mortgage rate you'll have to pay, as the lender is taking on more risk. This means your monthly repayments will be greater than those of a borrower who puts down a bigger deposit. So you could be better off by saving up for a bigger deposit and then qualifying for a lower interest rate on your mortgage.

Mortgage lenders usually set upper limits on the LTV ratio they will allow on each of their mortgage products, and the exact amount they lend will depend on several other factors.

For example, a buyer's age can affect how much money they may be able to borrow. Mortgages typically run for 25 years and lenders prefer to lend to borrowers who will be able to earn income during that period of time. They are less keen to lend to older borrowers, such as those approaching retirement or pensioners, and, as a result, if they do agree to provide mortgages to such borrowers, the lender will look to reduce the risk that the buyer will be unable to repay the loan by requiring a bigger deposit. The lender will want the loan repaid at a faster rate too, at a higher interest rate and over a shorter period of time. This makes repayments much more expensive each month.

One of the most important factors lenders take account of when deciding how much to lend – if at all – is a buyer's credit rating. If you have ever missed any payments on other loans or appear to be anything less than a thoroughly responsible borrower, a mortgage lender could reject your application or offer you a loan on less favourable terms, such as a higher interest rate.

So it's a good idea to view your credit report with one of the credit rating agencies such as Equifax or Experian. Some offer free trials and as long as you cancel before the end of the free-trial period, you'll be able to see your file at no cost. However, if you do have to pay, all the agencies are legally obliged to give you one-time access to your credit report for £2.

When you view it, check there are no mistakes; if there are, you can ask your financial providers to correct the information, which they are also obliged to do.

If you do have an impaired credit rating, there are simple steps you can take to boost your score, such as making sure you're on the electoral roll. If you have a limited credit history because you've never taken out a loan other than, say, a store card, you could take out a credit card at some point before you buy a home to prove to a mortgage lender you are able to manage your credit responsibly.

Organise your paperwork

Once you have worked out how much you can afford to spend, make sure your documentation is in order. Providing the following information on day one of your mortgage application can speed up the homebuying process no end.

Lenders typically like to see:

- your last three years' address history (with no gaps)

- your last three months' payslips

- your last three months' bank statements – some accept print-outs of online statements; others will ask for official copies, which can take up to two weeks to order from your bank

- your last P60 from your employer

- full details of any credit cards or loans – including interest-free furniture payments.

Don't hold anything back

When applying for a mortgage – either directly with the provider or through a financial adviser or mortgage broker – disclose any circumstances peculiar to your situation such as another income source or debt. If lenders are made aware of any irregularities early on, this will minimise delays and prevent your mortgage deal collapsing later on.

If you do have a peculiar situation, this is where financial advisers and mortgage brokers can really help, as they can advise on your personal circumstances and steer you away from applying for unsuitable mortgages.

However, if you do decide to use the services of such a professional, find out how much they will charge and which lenders' products they are able to recommend.

Independent advisers and brokers will be able to access the whole mortgage market, while others will be tied to a selection of lenders.

Parental support

If you have been gifted or are gifting a deposit, the money may need to be legally recognised, so mention it to your solicitor. They may require the person making the gift to sign legal documents stating that the money is indeed a gift, confirming that it is not to be repaid at any point and does not require a charge placed on the property (which means if you sell the property, you have to pay your creditor back from the proceeds of the sale). This can add to your legal costs.

Get an agreement in principle

Once you've got your finances in order, you should aim to get a mortgage agreement in principle (AIP). This confirms how much a lender will let you borrow, subject to it checking property-specific information such as valuation and survey results.

Securing an AIP before you start looking for a property will speed up the buying process as it will prove your creditworthiness and that you are a serious buyer to the estate agent and the seller. It also cuts out the wait in getting your mortgage application approved after you've made an offer on your chosen property, which can easily take a week, if not two.

Some borrowers like to get more than one AIP to find out if a different lender will loan them more money but mortgage brokers suggest getting AIPs from no more than two. This is because the credit checks the lenders perform to assess your mortgage application leave a trace on your credit history and too many checks can harm your credit rating, which could result in your application being rejected.

Making an offer

Once you have set your budget, have an AIP in place and have settled on your chosen property, it's time to make an offer to the seller. If the property is being marketed by an estate agent, you make an offer to the agent rather than to the seller directly.

There are no rules regarding a minimum amount to offer but in order to have your offer accepted, it must be fair and reflect local market conditions. For instance, if the type of property you want to buy is in short supply in the area and lots of buyers are interested in it, it is likely that only offers close to the full asking price (and often over it) will be considered.

When you're deliberating on how much to offer, you should also think about factors such as any work required to the property to bring it up to a suitable standard for your purposes. For instance, if you would need to install double glazing or central heating, you could deduct the likely cost from your opening offer price.

If you're buying a flat and it is a leasehold rather than a freehold flat, this will also help determine the kind of offer you might make. You could even negotiate money off by claiming it will cost you thousands to try to buy the freehold from the landlord.

If you find yourself in the position where you are not the only interested party and the seller has received an offer from another potential buyer, you will need to decide if you can afford to increase your original offer to secure the property.

Buying a home is an emotional purchase for many people and so, in this scenario, it can be easy to feel pressured into spending more money. But it is vital to remain cool, calm and objective. Don't be drawn into a bidding war. Go away and work out how much you can afford to make as a final offer, remembering that the more you up your offer by, the bigger your deposit will be, the more stamp duty you will pay and the higher your monthly mortgage repayments will be – a spur-of-the-moment higher offer could lead to years of financial stress.

How to calculate stamp duty

The stamp duty system was radically overhauled by Chancellor George Osborne in December 2014 when he delivered his Autumn Statement to parliament. He abolished the 'residential slab system' for paying stamp duty on property.

Since before the start of the millennium, stamp duty was charged at 1% for properties worth between £125,001 and £250,000, and then 3% on properties worth £250,001 to £500,000. That meant a stamp duty bill of £2,500 on a £250k home but £7,500 for one worth £250,001. As such, it was a hugely unpopular tax, which many homebuyers felt was unfair.

The new system for residential property, which came into force on 4 December 2014, works a bit like income tax. There's nothing to pay on the first £125,000 of the property's value but charges are levied on an ascending scale as the price rises.

A 2% charge is levied on the portion of a property value between £125,000 and £250,000. A 5% charge then applies to the portion of value that exceeds £250,000 up to £925,000. Between £925,001 and £1.5 million, a 10% charge kicks in and for everything above £1.5 million, a 12% charge is enforced.

If all those numbers are starting to make your head spin, here are some examples of what you would pay depending on different purchase prices.

1. At the time of writing, the average UK house price was £187,964, according to the Nationwide house price index. So a buyer would be liable to pay stamp duty on £62,964 (£187,964 minus the £125,000 exemption). For properties worth anything between £125,001 and £250,000, stamp duty is charged at 2%. So our buyer would face a stamp duty bill of £1,259.28 (2% of £62,964).

2. The average price in Hertfordshire was £349,271, so a buyer would be liable to pay stamp duty on £224,271 (£349,271 minus the £125,000 exemption). For the portion of the property value between £125,000 to £250,00, the 2% charge applies, which is £2,500 (2% of £125,000). For the remaining £99,271 chunk of the property value, the 5% charge applies, which equates to £4,963.55. So the total stamp duty payable is £2,500 plus £4,963.55, which is £7,463.55. Complicated, isn't it?

If you don't fancy giving the maths a go, HMRC has an online calculator tool you can use instead: **hmrc.gov.uk/tools/sdlt**

The Chancellor said 98% of homes paying stamp duty will be better off under the new system, which will result in a tax cut of £4,500 when buying a family home costing £275,000.

The new system initially applied to all of the UK but in April 2015 Scotland introduced one of its own.

The new Scottish stamp duty system

Called the land and buildings transaction tax (LBTT) and just like the new stamp duty system in place across England, Wales and Northern Ireland – it is a progressive system that charges homeowners proportionately more the higher the price of their property.

The first two rungs of the Scottish scheme are more generous than elsewhere in the UK. As for the first rung, there's no tax to pay on the first £145,000 of a property's value, compared to the less generous £125,000 under the UK system. This means that within the second rung (the 2% Scottish band between £145,001 and £250,000), a Scottish buyer of a £250,000 home would face a tax bill of just under £2,100, while their neighbours south of the border pay just under £2,500.

Between £250,001 and £325,000 a 5% levy applies. That's the same as the rest of the UK. But after this point, the Scottish system becomes a lot more expensive.

Properties selling for between £325,001 and £750,000 incur a 10% charge on the proportion of value over and above £325,001. That's in stark comparison with the UK system, where properties in that price bracket attract an additional 5% charge (the UK 10% rate doesn't apply until value exceeds £925,000). And while Scotland's maximum LBTT tax rate of 12% is the same as the rest of the UK's stamp duty rates, again it kicks in much sooner – at £725,001 compared to £1.5 million.

What happens after an offer is accepted?

This is when conveyancers get involved to begin the legal process of transferring ownership of the property from one person to another.

Some mortgage lenders allow you to instruct your own choice of conveyancer (solicitor), while others insist on you using a member of an approved 'panel'. Your estate agent should be able to recommend a local firm and when you get in contact for the first time, ask whether it can act for your particular mortgage lender.

It's a good idea to ask for two or three quotes for the legal work, with a breakdown of costs. Some solicitors will charge a flat rate, while others will charge a proportion of the asking price.

Individual costs can include the following:

EXPENSES	TYPICAL COST
The solicitor's professional fee	£600 plus VAT
Telegraphic transfer fee on completion for funds to the seller's solicitor	£30
Stamp duty (UK excluding Scotland)	Dependent on sale price*
	First £125,000: Zero
	Portion up to 2%: £250,000
	Portion up to 5%: £925,000
	Portion up to 10%: £1.5 million
	Above £1.5 million: 12%
Land Registry fee	Dependent on sale price: between £120 and £540 for properties sold for £100,000 to £1 million, or £910 for those more than £1 million
Plan	£6
Anti-money laundering search (per name)	£5
Full local search	£100
Water and drainage search	£55
Environmental search	£55
Chancel check	£18
Official search of the title (OS1)	£5

Stamp duty rates as of December 2014.

Don't forget that some costs will incur VAT on top at 20% and any legal complications with the purchase, such as a lease extension or gifted monies being used towards the deposit, can push the costs higher still.

It's also worth checking there will be no 'abortive fees' – costs you will have to pay even if the sale falls through. However, if your sale does fall through owing to factors beyond your control, most conveyancers will roll over any costs you did incur to your next purchase and won't charge you twice. Always ask for clarification of what would happen in this scenario before appointing a conveyancer.

When you've selected the solicitor you want to proceed with, you could ask them to agree to a fixed fee for the transaction. To give you confidence in the credentials of your conveyancer, visit **lawsociety.org.uk/accreditation** for a list of Conveyancing Quality Scheme accredited firms.

Surveys

The costs outlined above are not the only ones you'll have to fork out for. Once you have appointed a conveyancer, surveys can begin. There are three types that can be carried out and they vary in complexity and price.

Mortgage lender's valuation

The most basic is the mortgage lender's valuation, which all buyers are required to get. This survey does what it says on the tin – it assesses the property to check its valuation matches the amount of money the lender is being asked to provide a mortgage for.

Mortgage lenders will often cover the costs of the valuation as part of the overall cost of the mortgage, so borrowers don't have to pay separately upfront, but if your lender doesn't offer a so-called 'free' valuation, they typically cost between £150 and £300.

However, simply opting to go for the valuation survey could prove a false economy in the long run because they are usually based only on an external investigation of a property – or even a computerised valuation, without an inspection – and won't contain information about the property's condition. This could result in further costs if you subsequently have to correct any problems.

Homebuyer's Report

To find out more about the property, many buyers instead opt for the next survey up, a Homebuyer's Report. This costs between £300 and £500 and will provide information such as whether there is any damp in the property, what the insulation is like and if there's any subsidence. However, it won't provide information on issues such as how long it will be before the boiler might need replacing.

Full structural survey

The third type of survey is a full structural survey, which can cost around £1,000. This will uncover any major problems with the property, such as whether it may need a new roof. If problems are uncovered, a buyer can then decide whether they still want to proceed with the sale or whether to renegotiate the offer price. It can also help them avoid nasty and costly surprises once they move into the property.

How to choose a mortgage

According to the mortgage trade association, the Council of Mortgage Lenders, there are 11.1 million mortgages in the UK; if you put them all together, they're worth more than £1.2 trillion. When deciding on the right type of mortgage for you, there are two things you need to think about – how you want to repay it and the type of interest rate.

Most people choose repayment mortgages, where you pay back capital and interest every month. If all repayments are made in full, at the end of the mortgage term – typically 25 years – the borrower will own the property outright.

The other option is an interest-only mortgage. As its name suggests, repayments cover only the interest due on the original sum borrowed.

This makes the monthly repayments much cheaper than capital-and-interest (repayment) mortgages simply because you aren't repaying any of the capital. At the end of the mortgage term, the borrower does not own the property outright, so should they want to continue to live in it, they need to have an alternative way to clear the loan other than selling the property, such as cashing in equity investments.

Interest-only mortgages are suitable for only a limited number of buyers, including those who have good cause to expect their finances to improve significantly over a short period of time – for example, junior doctors, whose salaries rise quickly the more qualified they become, or those who earn large bonuses. Moreover, since the credit crunch, few mortgage lenders offer these mortgages.

So let's concentrate on repayment mortgages and the different options you have regarding the interest rate. You can choose either a fixed-rate or variable-rate mortgage.

Fixed-rate mortgages

In a nutshell, a fixed rate (or 'fix') gives certainty in that you know exactly how much your repayments will be during the period of the fix, which are widely available in two-, three- and five-year terms.

Fixed-rate mortgages are popular when people think the Bank of England's base rate – which influences all lenders' interest rates across the UK – is low or that it may rise. They want the certainty of locking themselves into a cheap rate for as long as possible to protect themselves should rates climb higher.

However, there's a price for certainty and so your monthly repayments will work out a little more expensive if you go for a fixed rate, compared to a variable rate.

Variable-rate mortgages

Variable-rate mortgages differ from their fixed-rate peers in that the interest rate you pay can go up and down from month to month. So while they don't offer any certainty, they do allow borrowers to benefit from cheaper mortgage repayments when interest rates fall or remain low.

There are three main types of variable mortgages – tracker rate, discounted rate and standard variable rate.

Tracker-rate mortgages

These rates move up and down (or track) in line with another interest rate, usually the Bank of England base rate, meaning that your monthly mortgage repayments can fluctuate. You pay less when rates fall and more when rates rise.

You can take out an introductory tracker rate for the first year, or even the first five years, of your mortgage. These introductory rates are frequently among the cheapest mortgage deals available but they often come with early repayment charges (a fee charged by your lender for changing the terms of your loan).

However, past the introductory period, most trackers don't tend to have early repayment charges and will let you make overpayments of up to 10% per year without penalty.

You can also go for a lifetime tracker where your mortgage will always be on a tracker rate.

Some lenders place a minimum limit on the interest rate to stop rates becoming unaffordable for them. However, if rates rise substantially, some trackers have what's known as a 'droplock' feature that lets you switch to one of your lender's fixed-rate mortgages, without paying an early repayment charge (although other fees may apply).

Discounted-rate mortgages

These usually offer a percentage point-style reduction on another interest rate – usually a lender's standard variable rate (SVR). Don't be fooled by the use of the word 'discount' and think that these are the cheapest mortgages available in terms of interest rate: they are not. The discount simply means that your payments might not be affected as much by rises in other interest rates. Your monthly mortgage repayments can still go up as well as down.

Like trackers, discounted rates are often available for an introductory period on your mortgage, during which time an early repayment charge will usually apply if you pay off the mortgage, or remortgage to another lender. However, generally overpayments of up to 10% of the outstanding balance per year are allowed and arrangement fees on discounted-rate mortgages are often cheaper than those on fixed- or tracker-rate deals.

Standard variable rate mortgage

You should think of the standard variable rate (SVR) as your mortgage lender's 'default' rate. At the end of a fixed, tracker or discount deal, your mortgage will normally revert to your lender's SVR.

It can rise and fall at any time and by a different amount from changes in the Bank of England base rate. They are cheap for the lender to run and so any fees attached to taking one out, or remortgaging to an SVR, are often very low and come with no early repayment charges should you want to repay your mortgage before the end of your mortgage term.

However, SVRs are usually more expensive than tracker and discounted rates.

Offset mortgages

If you have significant savings or a large balance on your current account, an offset mortgage that links your home loan to these accounts might be suitable for you.

Effectively, the money in your savings account is deducted from your mortgage and you have to pay interest only on the remainder. For example, if your mortgage debt is £200,000 and you have £25,000 in a savings account linked to your mortgage then you'll be charged interest on only £175,000 of the mortgage. Because you are paying less interest, you can repay your mortgage quicker.

While you have an offset mortgage, your savings won't earn interest so you will also cut your tax bill because you won't pay tax on interest earned. The higher the rate of income tax you pay, the more tax you stand to save. You'll also be able to access your savings should you really need to but you may increase your mortgage term or monthly repayments.

According to one offset mortgage provider, over recent years UK offset mortgage borrowers have been £1.4 billion better off than they would have been if they left the money they offset in best-buy savings accounts.

The problem with interest-only mortgages

Interest-only mortgages enable borrowers to repay only the interest on their loan, rather than both the interest and the capital, thereby significantly reducing monthly repayments. However, these mortgages have been plagued with problems and, today, lenders have much less appetite for them.

If you are in this situation, what can you do? The good news is that the banks recognise their responsibility to help borrowers develop realistic repayment strategies. So speak to your lender if you have any concerns to see what your options are.

If you can pay off some of your mortgage, reducing the loan to value (LTV) on your next mortgage, it will increase your choice of products. Alternatively, some lenders will let you take 50% of your new home loan on an interest-only basis and the rest on a repayment basis. This is a more affordable halfway house compared with switching to a repayment mortgage straightaway and will enable you to start building an equity stake in your home.

Remortgaging

Anyone with an existing mortgage can consider switching it to a better deal – from the same provider or a new one. The decision to remortgage is usually triggered by the existing mortgage's fixed-rate or discounted period coming to an end, a point at which most mortgage customers will automatically revert to their lender's SVR – which usually won't be competitive and will end up costing them more money each month.

Remortgaging has two main advantages – it enables you to save money and to raise money.

The way you save money is by getting a better deal that charges you a lower rate of interest on your home loan. For example, reducing the rate on a £150,000 loan over, say, a 15-year term from 5.5% to 4% would save you £116 a month.

Your chances of being able to secure a better rate by remortgaging are improved the more equity you build up in your home. For instance, a first-time buyer might have been able to afford only a 10% deposit when they bought their first home, so had a mortgage to cover the remaining 90% of the selling price. This means they owned 10% of the equity in their home and had a 90% LTV mortgage. However, five years later, at the end of their original mortgage's five-year fixed-rate period, a combination of having paid down some of the capital and house price growth could mean they now have 20% equity in their home. So when they look to remortgage, they will need only an 80% LTV mortgage, which will come with a lower rate than their original 90% LTV deal.

You can also raise money by remortgaging your home, again by taking advantage of the equity stake you have built up. Take this example: after ten years of paying off your original £200,000 mortgage, you have built up 50% equity – meaning you own £100,000 of your home. At this point, you have the option to remortgage to a 50% LTV deal that will secure you a lower interest rate. However, say you want to improve your home by adding an extension that will cost £20,000. You could remortgage to a deal that allows you to draw down 20% of the equity you've built up, giving you £20,000 in cash. So you then remortgage to a 60% LTV deal rather than a 50% deal. This means your remortgage will be for £120,000, rather than £100,000. Assuming your original mortgage was on a higher LTV than 60%, you could still save on the interest rate but have the added benefit of taking a cash lump sum.

Remortgaging usually takes about a month because you have your affordability assessed and have a valuation conducted on your home. When the process is complete, you'll be notified with a completion statement from your lender.

It's very important to find out if there will be any fees to pay when you remortgage. If you move lenders, expect to pay a charge to your old lender – which usually amounts to a few months' interest. You need to look at the numbers closely to make sure that any savings brought about by remortgaging to a better deal aren't wiped out by the accompanying charges.

You might also have to pay for legal fees and a property valuation to switch to a new lender, although some will give these for free or add them to your deal, so you don't always have to pay for them separately.

As with any mortgage, watch out for arrangement fees. Some come with fees of more than £1,000. And remember: the smaller the mortgage, the more important the fee.

Mortgage fees

When you're spending hundreds of thousands of pounds on a mortgage, it's easy to lose track of fees – a few hundred pounds can quickly start to feel like a drop in the ocean. However, fees vary greatly and can really stack up, so always find out exactly what costs come with a mortgage before you take out the loan.

There are three main types of fee to look out for. The first is the arrangement fee. This can go by other names, depending on the lender, such as a booking fee, reservation fee, completion fee or product fee. The fee covers the cost of the lender reserving the necessary funds for special deals such as fixed-rate or discounted-rate mortgages.

Some will state a specific amount – anything from £99 to £2,000 – while others will charge a proportion of the mortgage. Typically, the lower the mortgage rate, the bigger the fees and vice versa.

Arrangement fees either need to be paid for upfront or some lenders will allow you to add them to your mortgage. However, bear in mind that adding them to your mortgage works out more expensive in the long run, as you will pay more interest on your monthly repayments.

The second is legal fees, which cover the lender's cost of having to instruct a conveyancer to value the property. The price you pay is usually dependent on the price of the property. You will also have to pay fees to your own solicitor who will arrange all the legal work involved in buying a property. These will either be a set fee or a proportion of the house price.

The third fee to watch out for is an early-repayment charge, which you will normally have to pay if you decide to move your mortgage before the end of your introductory fixed, discounted or tracker deal.

The size of the fee is usually a percentage of the mortgage and how much you pay depends on the mortgage deal you signed up to and the size of your home loan. Alternatively, you may be charged extra interest. It's also worth remembering that you might have to repay any incentives you received for taking out your mortgage in the first place – such as free legal fees or cashback.

Buy-to-let mortgages

When you buy a home to live in, unless you are lucky enough to be a cash buyer you will need a residential mortgage. However, if you wish to buy property as an investment and plan to rent it out then you will need a buy-to-let mortgage. This is a 'commercial' mortgage, as the lender regards the purchase as a business transaction.

Buy-to-let mortgages are available from a wide range of lenders – from big high street banks to small specialist companies. Unlike residential mortgages, buy-to-let loans are not regulated by the Financial Conduct Authority and, as such, the lenders don't have to apply the tough affordability criteria brought into the residential market by 'The Mortgage Market Review' in March 2014 when assessing applications.

Buy-to-let mortgages tend to charge borrowers higher rates than those available on residential loans, and require bigger deposits, as they are deemed more risky. For instance, a homeowner is more likely to make sure they pay their mortgage or else they lose the roof over their heads. An investor isn't motivated by the same concern. And lenders also don't like the thought of 'void periods' – when the property sits empty between tenancies – in case the landlord struggles to cover the mortgage.

Sometimes homeowners become landlords 'accidentally'. Perhaps because they've tried to sell their home and can't achieve the price they require to stave off negative equity (the situation that arises when a property price falls below the outstanding mortgage). In such situations, they may be forced to rent out their home until prices have recovered.

If this happens to you, it is important to inform the mortgage lender as letting your home could breach your mortgage contract, which can have serious implications. For example, the lender could demand full and final repayment of the home loan, which would force many borrowers to default. Similarly, failing to notify your buildings and contents insurer could result in their refusing to pay out in the event of a fire.

Help for homebuyers

The government has several schemes to offer assistance to buyers – the most recent of which, Help to Buy, breaks from the norm and targets second-time buyers as well as those looking to buy their first property.

Here's a summary of some of the help available:

Help to Buy

Help to Buy has three parts. The first involves offering buyers of new-build properties (worth up to £600,000 in England and Northern Ireland) a five-year, interest-free equity loan from the government of up to 20% of the property value, provided that the buyers can raise a 5% deposit. This means the borrower needs to borrow only 75% of the property value from a mortgage lender, instead of 95%. This reduces the amount of risk the mortgage lender has to take on.

The equity loan from the government is interest-free for the first five years and then has an annual charge of 1.75%, rising each year by the Retail Prices Index (RPI) measure of inflation plus 1%.

You'll have to pay back the equity loan when you sell your home or at the end of your mortgage period, whichever comes first.

Help to Buy Scotland has its own equity loan arrangement for buyers of new-build properties. However, the property value cannot exceed £250,000. The Welsh version of the scheme, called Help to Buy Wales, sets the maximum property value at £300,000.

The mortgage lenders taking part in the scheme charge different fees for the loans and some will charge early-repayment fees. The Help to Buy deals aren't always the most competitive 95% loan-to-value (LTV) mortgages available, so bear this, and fees, in mind before signing up to the scheme.

The second part of Help to Buy sees the government provide a guarantee to underpin a borrower's mortgage, whether on a new-build or an older property in England, Wales, Scotland and Northern Ireland.

As long as the buyer can put down a 5% deposit on the value of their home, the government will guarantee a further 15% of the mortgage on properties worth up to £600,000 – again lowering the amount of risk the mortgage lender must take on.

The mortgage guarantee scheme is available to homebuyers across the UK but not to anyone buying a second home, or those who own property abroad.

The third part is the Help to Buy Isa, which was announced by the Chancellor in his March 2015 Budget. People saving to buy their first home will be given £50 for every £200 they save towards their deposit – up to a maximum bonus of £3,000. This means prospective first-time buyers need only save £12,000 in order to raise the average first-time buyer deposit of £15,000.

The smallest top-up the government will bestow is £400, which means the minimum amount a prospective homebuyer will need to save to qualify for the 25% top-up is £1,600.

The new accounts will be available through banks and building societies from autumn 2015 for four years but once an account has been opened there's no limit on how long people can save up for.

An initial deposit of up to £1,000 can be made upon opening the Isa and up to £200 can be saved monthly.

The Treasury has confirmed that the accounts will be limited to one per person rather than one per home "so those buying together can both receive a bonus".

Account openers must be at least 16 years old and buyers must be purchasing UK properties worth up to £450,000 in London, and up to £250,000 elsewhere. Would-be buyers must also not have opened a cash Isa within the same tax year.

The Help To Buy Isa top-up will be paid by voucher from the government to the mortgage lender upon the purchase of a home. The Isa cannot be used for buy-to-let property.

Shared ownership

Shared ownership is another type of scheme for new-build properties available throughout the UK, whereby first-time buyers can buy a share of the property – anything from 25% to 75% – while a housing association buys the rest.

The buyer then pays reduced rent to the housing association. Over time, the buyer can increase their share until they own the property outright, gradually reducing the amount of rent they pay.

The scheme is aimed at helping young people and low earners get on the property ladder, and it can be great for young professionals who are likely to see their earnings rise in the future.

There is a downside to shared ownership, however, in that the rent paid to the housing association can increase, which could make it harder to save enough money to increase your own share of the property. It can also be difficult to compare the interest rates and fees involved with these schemes, as there are no best-buy tables.

For more information on shared ownership schemes, visit **gov.uk/ shared-ownership-tenants**.

Five basic steps to buying a property

1. **Pre-contractual stage** Once an offer to buy is accepted, the seller's conveyancer draws up a contract, including details such as the selling price, what fixtures and fittings will be left in the property and the date for completing the purchase, known as 'completion'. The buyer's conveyancer then checks everything is correct. This is when surveys and valuations will be completed and buildings insurance arranged.

2. **Exchange of contracts** When the buyer and seller are happy with the contract, they sign final copies and send them to each other. The agreement is legally binding and neither party can pull out without paying compensation. A buyer usually pays the seller a deposit of about 10% of the purchase price at this point, and this is usually held by the conveyancer until completion.

3. **Between exchange and completion** A few more checks will be done by the conveyancers at this stage, such as making sure they have all the necessary funds, and they will then arrange for the transfer of funds to the seller.

4. **Completion** The money for the property is transferred from buyer to seller and the keys and legal documents are handed over. The property now belongs to the buyer.

5. **After completion** The buyer's conveyancer registers the change of ownership with HM Land Registry, the buyer pays stamp duty and has to inform their insurer that completion has taken place.

Selling your home

When it comes to selling your home, you need to try your best to leave sentimentality to one side. Just because you loved your scarlet red bedroom doesn't mean prospective buyers will. Being practical and realistic will stand you in much greater stead, saving you time and perhaps even making you money.

BUYING AND SELLING PROPERTY

Setting the asking price

The most important thing will be to get the asking price right. Do your homework by thoroughly researching the local market. You could start off by looking at sold prices in your area on the Land Registry website (**houseprices.landregistry.gov.uk**), where you can find recent sales data by postcode or street address for properties in England and Wales. You'll also find a house price calculator that will give you a rough idea of how much prices have changed over the years.

Choosing an agent – costs and contracts

A good estate agent should be able to give you the most accurate price, using their knowledge of the intricacies of your local housing market. They are also incentivised to sell your house as quickly as possible for as much money as they can, because they usually charge a fixed percentage of the sale price as their fee (which can vary from 0.75% to 3% – so £1,500 to £6,000 on a £200,000 sale price). If your house fails to sell, they don't get paid.

While it's in your interest for your home to secure the highest possible sale price, plumping for an agent based solely on the highest price can be risky. If a buyer thinks it's overpriced, they'll either make an offer at significantly less than the asking price or, worse still, they won't bother viewing your house at all. So when choosing an agent, ask several for valuations and settle on a fair price.

You should also find out how long they will market your property for and exactly what level of service they will provide. For instance, traditional estate agents tend to arrange professional photographs and Energy Performance Certificates (a legal obligation for sellers), draw up floorplans, erect 'for sale' boards and conduct viewings as standard. However, online agents (who usually charge lower fees but take the money upfront and normally keep it regardless of whether your house sells) charge extra for these things.

Also, spend time carefully reading the contract before signing it. This is where you'll find information such as whether a "sole agency lock-in period" applies. This means the agent wants to market your home exclusively for a certain period of time, barring you from listing your home with other agents. These lock-in periods vary by agent but can be anything from four to 12 weeks – if you sign a contract with one agent who has such a lock-in clause but sell your home via another agent instead, you could face paying two sets of commission fees.

Show your home at its best

To make your property appeal to as many buyers as possible, follow these simple tips:

- Declutter: hiding away untidy piles of belongings can make your home look bigger

- Fix and clean: repair anything unsightly such as holes in the walls and clean everything

- Tidy the garden: mow the grass, do the weeding.

PART 2:
Save Money

Get rid of debt

Before you can see any real benefit from saving, you need to get rid of as much debt as possible. After all, there's really no point regularly transferring money into a savings account paying a couple of per cent in interest if, for example, your outstanding credit card balance is costing you almost ten times as much.

This is not to say that you have to be entirely debt-free before you can start to save or that debt is necessarily bad. Indeed, access to credit and the ability to spread payments is a very useful way of managing your money. But the big risk of credit is that borrowers fall behind with repayments and the original debt increases as the interest charged on it by the lender stacks up.

This is why, if you can, you should always look to pay your balance in full at the earliest opportunity. If you can't, to stop your debt from becoming unmanageable, there are strategies you can put in place.

Credit cards

There are three simple rules for paying off credit cards.

1. Always repay what you owe on the card charging the highest annual percentage rate (APR) first. The longer the balance goes unpaid, the more it will cost you to eventually clear.

2. Transfer your balance – this means moving all your credit card balances to a card with a smaller APR. You can do this by taking out a balance-transfer deal. Typically, you'll be able to transfer your outstanding credit card debt to a card that won't charge any interest at all on new balances for up to 24 months (or more in

some cases) but you will be charged a fee of around 3% of the balance you want to transfer.

Don't ignore repayments – a debt of £1,000 on a credit card charging an APR of 17.56% (the average APR charged on credit cards for the year ending 31 July 2013 according to the Bank of England) would cost a borrower £14.63 in interest a month. But if they were to switch it to a balance-transfer card deal where the balance would be interest-free for six months, even with a 3% fee they'd pay just £30 for the convenience of freezing it for six months – a saving of nearly £58 compared to the interest they would have been charged had they left the £1,000 balance sitting on the 17.56% APR card.

Use comparison websites to find the best balance-transfer credit card deals.

3. Set up a direct debit for at least the minimum repayment to make sure you never miss a payment – most credit card providers will charge you for late or missed payments and these can also adversely affect your credit score.

Personal loans

Personal loans let you borrow more money upfront than credit cards, and the interest rate is usually lower because the loan is secured against your property (meaning your home could be at risk if you fail to repay your loan). However, unlike a credit card (which is an unsecured loan), a personal loan is arranged for a set period of time – often three, five or seven years – and repayments are split equally over the term of the loan. You can't just pay the minimum amount off each month, like you can with a credit card.

So, in this sense, a personal loan effectively comes with its own repayment strategy set by the lender. This should make it easier for you to budget too, as you always know exactly what your repayment amount will be.

It is always best to arrange a loan for the shortest time possible. While this will make your monthly repayments bigger, it will prevent you paying more in interest over the term of the loan.

If you find yourself in the fortunate situation of being able to repay your loan early, before you do, find out if an early-repayment charge will apply: depending on the term of your loan, it may be cheaper to stick to the original repayment schedule.

If you think there's a good chance that you will be able to repay it, you might find a flexible loan more suitable for your needs. A flexible loan can usually be taken out for up to a year and interest rates vary from 5% to 18%. The general rule of thumb is the shorter the term of the loan, the higher the interest rate. The advantage of a flexible loan over other short-term loans is that it allows you to repay the money more quickly than originally agreed without penalty.

Payday loans

If you need access to a relatively small amount of money for a very short period of time and are unable to get it from your bank in the form of an authorised overdraft, or you can't take out an interest-free credit card – perhaps because you have a poor credit score – there are other ways to borrow money. However, the price you will pay for the convenience of short-term credit is a much higher interest rate.

Some people who need to borrow money for a few days until they get paid turn to payday loans. These charge significantly higher interest rates than any other form of borrowing. They are designed to last for very short periods of time – usually less than a month.

As part of the agreement, lenders often require the borrower to allow them to take the repayments straight from their bank account through what is called a 'continuous payment authority'.

If borrowers become unable to stick to the repayment schedule, the lender may agree to extend the loan (known as a 'rollover') but will usually increase the interest rate during the extension and might charge additional fees.

Payday loans are a controversial form of borrowing and lenders have been widely criticised for exploiting vulnerable consumers. The critics argue that, all too often, payday loans exacerbate the problems of those in debt by recklessly lending to individuals who are unable to repay the loan on time and then end up paying more interest than originally expected.

Until April 2014, the industry was largely unregulated and not all lenders had strict affordability criteria in place when deciding who to lend money to. Some payday loans came with sky-high APRs.

However, in November 2014 payday lenders were forced to slash the interest rates and fees they charge borrowers when its regulator, the Financial Conduct Authority (FCA), stepped in to clean up the market. It ruled that borrowers must never be forced to repay more than twice what they originally borrowed.

In other words, if you borrow £100, in the worst-case scenario you can only ever be forced to repay £200. While still expensive, effective interest rates of 100% represent a significant reduction compared to previous industry norms where the likes of Wonga charged more than 5,000% APR.

Payday lenders also have to comply with a daily cap on interest of 0.8%, so someone borrowing £100 over 30 days would repay a rate of 80p per day, or £24 in total. Borrow £500, and that's £4 a day or £120 a month.

Other measures that have been introduced include a £15 cap on default charges and limiting the number of times a loan can be rolled over to two.

Lenders have also been restricted in the number of times they can dip into a borrower's bank account (via a continuous payment authority) to seek payment to two. They must also conduct a mandatory affordability check for every loan.

BEWARE PAYDAY LOAN BROKERS

It's crucial to make sure you know exactly what you are signing up for when it comes to taking out a payday loan. A lot of companies advertising quick loans online are not actually payday lenders but brokers. These are businesses that effectively refer your application information on to loan firms in return for a hefty fee.

Short–term borrowers are increasingly being duped into unwittingly agreeing to fees levied by these brokers, either through not checking the terms and conditions or the T&Cs not being clear enough. The Financial Ombudsman Service (FOS) says it has seen a huge rise in recent complaints about brokers that drain money from people's accounts without providing them with the loan they were looking for. It was contacted by more than 10,000 people complaining about broker websites in the first eight months of 2014 alone. In two-thirds of cases it investigated, the FOS found that the consumer had been treated unfairly.

While credit brokering is a legitimate activity, under the Consumer Credit Act all firms are required to display all fees and charges prominently so as to not misinform the consumer.

Consolidating debt

Having significant personal debt puts your family finances at risk. What if you were to lose your job or become unable to work? Would you be able to continue to pay your bills? If you are concerned about your debt, it may be worth turning to a debt-consolidation loan or, if you are a homeowner, a home equity loan to clear all your debts at once.

If you have several debts with different lenders, you might want to take out a single loan to consolidate your borrowings. A consolidation loan will give you money to pay off your outstanding debts – which could include credit cards, store cards or personal loans. It can make it easier to manage your finances as you have to make only one monthly payment and it can save you money if it charges you less interest than you pay on your existing debt.

However, while it could reduce your monthly payments, you could end up repaying your debt more slowly. Moreover, if the duration of the consolidation loan is longer than that of your other debts, you could end up paying more in total than had you not combined your loans, as your debt will accrue interest for longer.

Alternatively, you could make higher monthly repayments and clear your consolidated loan more quickly, reducing the overall cost. Just watch out for early-repayment fees you may have to make to the lender to make up for some of the interest it will lose.

If you are a homeowner with equity in your property, a home equity loan could also help you to consolidate your debt. These loans allow you to borrow against the equity in your home and you can then use the money to consolidate your other debts. The home equity loan provider uses your home as security (making these loans a type of secured borrowing), which can be risky if you fail to keep up with repayments. However, the interest rates it will charge on home equity loans are often lower than unsecured loans.

If you want to tackle your debt yourself, you'll need to know which debt to sort out first.

Priority debt

You should always rank your debt in order of importance and it's not always as simple as prioritising the most expensive debt first. Top-priority debts should be those that affect your home, your capacity to earn a living or those that might lead to criminal prosecution if you fail to repay them.

If your debt becomes significant and you find yourself unable to repay all of it because of, say, redundancy or ill health, you may need to 'triage your debt'.

'Triage' is the term used by accident and emergency departments of hospitals; it is what military doctors do on the battlefield when they know they can save only some of their patients, not all. To triage is to prioritise which health cases are the most urgent – or who can be saved on the battlefield, if you like. You can do the same with your debts.

Highest priority

Secured debt, such as your mortgage, should always be your top priority. If you fail to keep up these repayments, you could lose your home. The same applies to your rent.

Next in the pecking order should be gas and electricity bills, as failure to repay these could see you lose the energy supply to your home.

Then come Council Tax arrears. If you don't keep up with these payments, your local authority can go to court to enforce the debt.

Court fines such as penalties for driving offences are next. If you don't pay these, the creditor can get a court order to arrest your wages or freeze your bank account. If, after this, you still have unpaid arrears, you can be sent to prison.

The same goes for maintenance payable to an ex-partner or children. This includes child maintenance you owe to the Child Support Agency or Child Maintenance Service.

You can also be sent to prison for failure to pay income tax or VAT. And it is a criminal offence to use a television without a valid TV licence, which can lead to prosecution, a court appearance and a fine of up to £1,000 (excluding legal costs).

Other high-priority debts include any you have for goods you rely upon. These could include your car if you're disabled and rely on it for mobility, or if you need your car to run your business. If you bought your car through a hire-purchase agreement and fall behind with your repayments, it could be repossessed.

Dealing with creditors

If you are struggling to repay your debts, you should contact the companies you owe money to as soon as possible and explain your situation. It may be that your inability to repay is short-term – for example, you've been off work because you are unwell. If your lender knows and understands that your situation will soon improve (you will shortly be able to return to work, for example, or claim benefits) it may agree to give you a payment holiday or allow you to reduce your repayments.

You could also work out what you could afford to repay, albeit over a longer time period, and ask your lender to consider adjusting your repayment schedule. Remember: all a lender wants is to get its money back, so it's in its interest that you can afford the repayments.

However, if your debt is significant, you will need to inform your creditors what you think you may be able to repay – if anything. You may have to do this formally through a debt management plan (DMP).

Debt management plan

A DMP is an agreement between you and the companies to which you owe money to pay all of your debts. Such a plan can be used to pay only unsecured debts. You make regular payments to a licensed debt management company, which then shares this money between your creditors.

You should set up a plan only with a debt management company licensed by the Financial Conduct Authority (FCA) and, ideally, you should find one via a specialist debt charity, as there are rogue companies operating in this field. The company will work out your monthly payments based on your financial situation, including your assets, debts, income and creditors.

The company then contacts your creditors on your behalf and asks them to agree to the plan (they aren't obliged to do so). Some debt managers will charge you a set-up fee as well as a handling fee every time you make a payment. You should be made aware of any charges before signing up for a debt management service.

Your plan can be cancelled if you don't keep up your repayments – see page 81 for more help.

Administration order

If you have a county court or High Court judgment against you, which you can't pay in full, an administration order may help.

The court will decide how much of your debt you have to repay, how much your monthly repayments will be and how long the arrangement will last. You will make one payment a month to your local court, which will split the money between your creditors. You'll pay a court fee each time you make a repayment, capped at 10% of your debt.

To be eligible, you must owe less than £5,000, including any interest and charges, owe money to at least two creditors and prove you can afford your repayments.

If you fail to keep to the terms of the agreement, the court can deduct money from your wages and cancel the arrangement. Your administration order will be made public and added to the Register of Judgments, Orders and Fines, and will remain there for six years.

To apply for an administration order, you need to fill in an N92 form, which you can download online at **hmctscourtfinder.justice.gov. uk**, and return it to your local court.

Extreme debt

Individual voluntary arrangements

If you have built up substantial debts that you are unable to pay but want to stave off bankruptcy, you could enter into an individual voluntary arrangement (IVA). Similar to how administration orders work for those unable to pay county court judgments (CCJs), IVAs work by enabling the debtor to pay off a portion of their total debts over a manageable time period. At the end of the agreed period, the rest of their debt is cancelled.

IVAs are negotiated with creditors by an independent insolvency practitioner (IP), who acts on behalf of the debtor. The IP will receive either a percentage of the amount repaid, or a flat fee.

IVAs may be more preferable to some debtors than bankruptcy as there is not so much stigma attached and they won't have to deal with some of the practical consequences of bankruptcy.

Bankruptcy

If you have debts that you are simply unable to repay and your situation is unlikely to change in the foreseeable future, you may have no choice but to declare yourself bankrupt.

Bankruptcy is a court order you can apply for if you are in debt. However, the people to whom you owe money (a £750 minimum applies but this will rise to £5,000 from October 2015) can also apply to make you bankrupt even if you don't want to do so yourself.

Once you have been made bankrupt, an 'Official Receiver' (an officer of the bankruptcy court) takes control of your finances, including any assets you may have, such as your home, and deals with your creditors so you don't have to.

After your bankruptcy order is over, the money you owe is usually written off, meaning that your creditors have to stop trying to get their money back. Usually, you'll be able to wipe the slate clean after one year.

However, bankruptcy is no easy solution. It must be carefully considered as it comes with serious long-term implications for your finances and career prospects. First, although it sounds ridiculous, you have to pay fees of £705 to go bankrupt and so not all debtors can afford to do it. (Citizens Advice can tell you about any charities in your area that can help pay the fees. Visit **citizensadvice.org.uk** for more information.)

Your bankruptcy will also be made public and the news will be posted in your local paper, as well as *The London Gazette* and on the Insolvency Service website (**www.gov.uk/government/ organisations/insolvency-service**).

You will be disqualified from running a business and you can be banned from practising in certain professions such as some roles within financial services. In addition, your ability to borrow money again in future will be very limited.

You should also bear in mind that the bankruptcy procedure doesn't get rid of some debts such as court fines, student loans and child maintenance.

Debt relief order (DRO)

A DRO is a low-cost alternative to bankruptcy for people with very low incomes, who do not own their own home and who have debts they are unlikely to repay. The official receiver's fee is £90.

To be eligible, you must owe less than £15,000 (rising to £20,000 in October 2015), have spare income of less than £50 a month and assets worth less than £300.

If you get a DRO, your creditors won't be able to recover their money without the court's permission and you'll usually be freed from your debts after 12 months. You will also be subject to certain restrictions during the year, including not being able to borrow more than £500 without telling the lender about your DRO or act as the director of a company.

Your DRO will be added to the Individual Insolvency Register and will be removed three months after it ends. It will stay on your credit record for six years.

If you're worried about debt, these debt advice websites offer free help:

- **debtadvicefoundation.org**
- **moneyadviceservice.org.uk**
- **nationaldebtline.org**
- **stepchange.org**

Set yourself a goal

First off, give yourself a pat on the back. If you're ready to seriously begin saving for a new car, home, holiday or wedding, it means you must be in control of your finances. So you must be financially savvy and the envy of your debt-ridden friends.

That said, if you do still have credit card debt or a personal loan, it may well be worth paying this off before you start to save: there's no point paying sky-high interest on debt if you can pay it off early and begin saving that extra cash.

So why do we save? After all, if you want to get married, you could just stick the cost on a credit card and worry about it later. You can do that, of course, and we detail the lowest-cost options available to you in our chapter on getting married (see page 103). But the most sensible among you will save for the event and avoid having to service expensive debt long after your big day has come and gone.

It's the same for anything you wish to buy: you can buy it on credit and pay for it later, or you can save and buy it when you can actually afford it. Credit cards with 0% interest rates aside, this remains the most sensible option. Save first, buy later. Our parents and grandparents did it that way, and it remains the ideal.

Whatever it is you wish to save for, you'll need to set yourself a goal – a date by which you wish to have saved enough to buy what you want. If it's a wedding, that should be pretty easy but if it's, say, a new car, tell yourself that you want to buy it on such and such a date, and make that the end goal. By having goals and targets, you'll have something tangible to work toward, and imagine how good you'll feel when you finally splash out on what you saved for.

Cut your costs

It can be a good idea to cut your costs before you begin saving; it will get you in the habit of being thrifty and maximise the amount you can put aside each month. You need to think about budgeting, paying less for things and being financially savvy about your household bills.

The first step is to create a household budget. It will allow you to see where you are spending your money and where you need to cut back.

It's easier than ever these days, as modern technology can do the hard work for you. You can even do it on the go through smartphone apps, meaning you can stay on top of your finances wherever, whenever. For example, the free Toshl app (available on iPhone and Android) allows you to input your income along with expenses to ensure you stay within your budget and will export what you've created straight to your computer. Alternatively, search online for a household budget template – there are lots of them.

Budgeting will also give you the chance to see if you have any extra cash in your current account, which could work harder for you. For example, you could 'sweep' the extra cash into a savings account that pays more interest. You can set this up automatically, so that at the end of each month, your bank will take whatever is left above a certain limit and transfer it into your savings account.

Cut your bills

There are still far too many consumers paying over the odds on their household bills, particularly energy. At the time of writing, the average household energy bill is nudging £1,200 a year and yet six in ten households have never switched energy suppliers, according to comparison website uSwitch. If you're one of them, then you could be missing out on hundreds of pounds by choosing the wrong energy tariff. uSwitch claims that the difference between the cheapest and the most expensive providers can be in excess of £200 a year.

The most expensive tariffs are suppliers' old-fashioned standard tariffs, especially the variable tariffs that are paid by cash or cheque. However, most energy experts claim that fixed-price tariffs are better value, as they allow people to fix their prices, thereby protecting themselves from any future price hike, while also saving money.

So ditch and switch. First, check exactly what tariff you're currently on; then, use a comparison website to check what you're paying against rival suppliers. The comparison site will even help you handle the switch, so there's no excuse for paying more than you should.

The same goes for broadband, home phone and any TV deals you might be on: always keep track of the market and, after checking you won't incur any penalties for leaving your existing deal before a certain date, if you find you are paying over the odds, switch.

Cashback

Another good habit to get into is to take advantage of cashback schemes. There are lots of ways to effectively get paid to spend, on everything from food and clothes to your utility bills. For example, Santander's 123 current account (costing £2 a month) pays 1% cashback on water bills and Council Tax. It pays the same on Santander mortgage payments up to £1,000, 2% on energy bills, and 3% on mobile, home phone, broadband and TV packages.

Similarly, RBS and NatWest operate a cashback scheme for existing and new current account customers, which pays 1p for every £1 spent on a debit card. Even better, it's free to register for.

You could also get money back from cashback websites, such as Quidco or Top Cashback. They work by giving you a cut of the commission they receive when you buy something from a huge variety of online retailers via their cashback sites. You can register for free.

Vouchers

As the economy hit the skids in 2008, the UK went discount mad as a way to stretch ever-tightening budgets. These days, no one thinks twice about visiting a restaurant such as Pizza Express (especially mid-week) without first looking for an online discount voucher.

As a result, a huge array of voucher code websites, such as **vouchercodes.co.uk** and **vouchercloud.com**, started popping up.

There are also group buying sites such as Groupon and Living Social (which work by offering cheap deals as a certain number of buyers snap up the deal). The voucher game is now big business.

As a nation, we like vouchers so much that research by Webloyalty has found that nearly half (47%) of Brits have now used discount vouchers, with 30% of us using them for leisure activities, such as going to the cinema, while 28% have used them to book a holiday.

However, you have to be choosy as many discount sites are filled with special offers for things we often don't need, or want very often, such as teeth whitening, carpet cleaning and spray tans. Moreover, many deals are available only on certain days or for a very limited time, so it can be tricky to use a voucher before it expires.

The voucher market has improved in other areas, for example with the emergence of apps. These allow smartphone and tablet users to find discounts or vouchers on the move. As they use geo-location technology, people are able to see only vouchers that will work in shops and restaurants nearby.

Loyalty schemes

It comes as little surprise that most stores have cottoned on to the fact customers like being rewarded for their loyalty. It makes us feel valued and will more than likely keep us returning to the shop time and time again; if used sensibly, they can also help cut our shopping costs.

Loyalty cards, such as Tesco's Clubcard and the Nectar card, reward customers with a number of points for every pound spent, which can then be exchanged for vouchers or discounts. The benefits vary greatly from card to card.

But loyalty cards are not on offer out of the goodness of retailers' hearts; they are carefully calculated schemes to get the most out of each customer, which makes using them properly all the more important.

If you spend your points almost as quickly as you earn them, you won't really see much benefit or a lot of savings, so you should aim to let your points build up as long as you can.

Here's how the UK's three major schemes work.

Tesco Clubcard: offers one point for every £1 spent across a range of products, from in-store and online to more niche departments, such as motoring and travel. Tesco fuel will earn you a point for every £2 spent and there are more points on offer for those using a Tesco Clubcard credit card. A total of 150 points equals a £1.50 shopping voucher, and each £5 voucher equals £20 in reward vouchers, which can be used with companies including Pizza Express and Avios, the airmile scheme.

Clubcard points can be used for discounts on flights, hotels and package holidays, days out at places such as Alton Towers, and a wide range of brands. Customers will often get more for their points if they pay with a Tesco Clubcard credit card.

With the Clubcard's rewards scheme, you can exchange a number of points for different products. For example, £8 worth of points can be exchanged for a ticket to Madame Tussauds in London. There is a host of other days out and restaurants to use your vouchers on.

Nectar card: offers one point for every £1 spent in-store and online at Sainsbury's, plus a point for every £1 spent on petrol.

Nectar points can also be earned at other retailers, including Homebase, British Gas and eBay, at varying rates.

As for redeeming points, 500 equals £2.50 to spend, and the same figure applies for offers at most companies participating in the scheme, from Bella Italia to easyJet and even Oxfam.

The Nectar card boasts the greatest range of companies through which you can earn your points, from Expedia to Vision Express, and a similar offering to Tesco for the sort of places where you can spend your points, as well as a special section online where points can be exchanged for magazine subscriptions, meals out and even charitable giving. For example, 5,000 points (worth £25) buys an Oxfam Unwrapped gift of a goat for an impoverished family.

Again, customers will benefit more if they hold a Nectar credit card, while businesses can sign up for a Nectar Business credit card and earn points on business expenditure.

Boots Advantage card: returns four points for every £1 spent in-store, online and at Boots Opticians. Each point is worth 1p and can be spent in-store and online. Its Parenting Club also gives families ten points for every £1 spent on baby products. The Boots Advantage card probably offers the fewest outlets through which you can spend your points, although it has an exclusive 'Treat Street' where you can receive one-off offers for a range of shops, such as B&Q and Matalan. However, its standard four-points-to-a-£1 ratio makes this card a must-have for shoppers.

Savings accounts

So now that you've paid off your debts, you're budgeting effectively and using vouchers when you shop or treat yourself, you are ready to begin saving.

First off, you'll need to choose somewhere to save your money, as leaving the extra in your current account could be a mistake: while savings rates are poor at the moment, many current accounts don't pay any interest at all on balances in credit.

So how do you pick the best savings account? The key is to consider what you need from the account and how you want it to work for you. Remember that, ideally, you want to find an account that beats inflation, otherwise the real value of your savings will be eroded by increases in the cost of living.

Safeguard your savings

If you have a lot of money to save, you'll need to give some thought to what would happen if the provider were to go bust. Regulated banks and building societies offer a degree of protection to savers because 100% of the first £85,000 you have in a savings account is protected by the Financial Services Compensation Scheme (FSCS).

However, this limit applies to each banking group, not each individual bank; because some banks are part of the same banking group, you could get caught out should the worst happen. For example, HSBC and First Direct are part of HSBC Bank. So make sure you don't inadvertently exceed the £85,000 limit when selecting your savings account.

Finally, make the most of your circumstances. Joint accounts are protected up to £170,000, so couples can get away with saving more in one place without jeopardising their protection.

Choosing an account

Easy- or instant-access accounts are ideal if you need to get at your cash without giving notice or having interest reduced. These are also perfect for rainy day or emergency funds. The downside is they don't pay the highest rates.

Regular saver accounts reward monthly deposits with rates that are better than instant-access accounts. However, you must pay in every month and you can't usually access the money for a year.

Fixed-rate accounts or bonds pay a set rate of interest for a given term – usually one to five years – but you will get less if you withdraw money during this time (see more on fixed-rate bonds on page 94). As you're tying up your money, you are likely to earn a higher rate. However, you may not want to lose access to your money for too long because if interest rates rise, the account may start looking less competitive.

A halfway house is a notice account, which locks your money away and requires 'notice' (usually between one and three months) to access it in return for higher rates.

Once you know the type of account you need – and that may be more than one – don't head straight to your bank. You may have had a current account with it for years but that doesn't mean that it will give the best rates for your savings. Instead, shop around using comparison websites. Some top rates of interest are there only to

SET YOURSELF A GOAL

attract you and will drop after a few months, so think about longer-term and fixed rates, particularly if you're locking your savings away.

Individual savings accounts (Isas)

Whichever type of account you go for, you should always make the most of your individual savings account (Isa) allowance as a long-term savings strategy.

Each tax year, money can be paid in and held in cash or be invested in stocks and shares. The interest you earn, and any gains you make, are tax-free. And if you don't need to dip into your savings, the interest you earn boosts your original deposit over time, providing a greater base from which to grow. This is known as compound interest and works as follows:

In year one, an account paying 5% will pay £50 on a £1,000 deposit, but in year two it will pay £52 because that 5% is being applied to a new bigger balance of £1,050. As each year passes the more your money will grow.

How much money can be paid into an Isa changes on a yearly basis. In July 2014, the government rebranded Isas 'New Isas' or 'Nisas' and significantly increased the amount that could be held in any combination across cash and stocks shares Isas to £15,000, up from a little over £11,000 (when the full amount could only be held in stocks and shares, and only half could be held in cash). In the 2015/16 tax year, which started on 6 April 2015, the limit has risen to £15,240.

NB: the financial community has failed to adopt the 'New Isa' moniker so we'll call them Isas throughout the book.

Cash Isas

These accounts have proved very popular thanks to their ability to shield savings interest from tax. Up until now, basic-rate taxpayers have had to pay income tax of 20% on the interest their savings outside an Isa have generated. For example, if they put £1,000 in a normal savings account paying 3%, the money would generate interest of £30 over a year but they'd only get £24 after tax (their bank or building society automatically deducted the tax). For a higher-rate taxpayer, paying tax on interest at 40%, the return falls to £18. But if either taxpayer held their £1,000 in a cash Isa instead, they would receive the full £30.

Although this may be a difference of only a few pounds, over time this can add up. For instance, assuming interest rates remain at 3% and you don't add any more money to your account, in an Isa your £1,000 will have grown to £1,159 after five years. A basic-rate taxpayer using a taxed account would have £1,126, while a higher-rate taxpayer would have £1,093.

However, from April 2016, 95% of UK taxpayers will no longer have to pay tax on savings interest at all, according to the Treasury. In the Chancellor's Budget in March 2015, George Osborne announced the introduction of the annual Personal Savings Allowance that will make the first £1,000 of interest earned from savings completely tax-free for basic-rate taxpayers from April 2016. You would have to have £50,000 in an account paying 2% to generate £1,000 of interest (gross) a year. Higher-rate taxpayers will also have an allowance but this is lower at £500.

The allowance means anyone earning up to £42,700 (basic-rate taxpayers) and enjoying interest on their non-Isa savings of, say, £800, would be able to keep it all tax-free. But should the interest amount to, say, £1,200, then they would have to pay tax on £200 over and above the maxium £1,000 allowance. Similarly, those earning £42,701 to £150,000 and receiving savings interest of £800 would enjoy the first £500 of it tax-free but would have to pay tax on the remaining £300.

While the changes mean that there won't be any real difference between cash Isas and normal savings accounts in terms of tax treatment from one year to the next, for basic-rate taxpayers – as mentioned above – it is over the long-term that Isas will really come into their own. If you're fortunate enough to be able to use your full annual Isa allowance, it will only take you four years to build up a £50,000 pot that could generate the maximum personal savings allowance of £1,000 interest (gross, assuming a 2% interest rate).

As for the running of an Isa, although some allow you to pay money in one day and withdraw it the next, if you do take money out you won't be able to replace that part of your Isa allowance for the rest of the current tax year. However, this rule – which has been in place since the introduction of Isas in 1999 – is being scrapped in autumn 2015. So people will be able to repay in any money they withdraw within the same tax year.

But changes aside, remember that when picking the right Isa for you, the first thing to decide is whether you want to fix your interest rate or opt for more flexibility with a variable rate. If you want to secure the interest rate you earn on your savings and are happy to lock your money away for a set period of time, then a fixed-rate Isa might be for you. However, if you want to make additional deposits beyond the upfront opening deposit or make withdrawals, then an easy-access Isa would be more suitable.

Stocks-and-shares Isas

You can also invest your Isa allowance in stocks and shares. The money you deposit into the account is invested in the stock market. The aim of this is to generate a higher rate of return over the medium to long term than can be achieved through interest alone. However, the price of that potential to generate a higher rate of return is taking on risk. Over the long term, the stock market usually outperforms cash but while history proves this to be the case, future performance cannot be guaranteed.

Unlike Isa money held in cash, the value of money invested in stocks and shares can fall as well as rise and you could get back less than you put in. So individuals with short-term savings goals, who may need access to the money within, say, five years, might be better suited to keeping their Isa money in cash. Those with longer-term savings objectives – such as helping their children buy a home when they grow up – are better suited to stocks and shares because they have time to ride out any short-term volatility.

That said, you don't need to pick between the two: you can do both. Savers can put up to £15,240 a year into Isas – you can pay into no more than one cash account and one stocks-and-shares account in any tax year – and they can decide to do so in any combination they choose.

How to transfer an Isa

You don't have to stick with the same account provider(s) year in, year out. Whether you want a better rate, are fed up with poor service or want to move money between cash and stocks and shares, you can move previous year's Isas to a new provider. You can also shift cash Isas during the tax year.

If you choose to open a new account, it's important to follow the Isa transfer rules as you'll lose your tax-free benefits if you withdraw the money and redeposit it yourself.

Instead, speak to your new Isa provider, which will be able to manage the transfer process on your behalf. It will ask you to complete an application form to open one of its Isas and a transfer form to enable it to request the money from your existing Isa provider.

It's important to remember that different rules apply depending on whether you want to transfer the current year's Isa allowance or that of a previous year. If you're moving money you've paid in during this tax year, you will need to move it all to a new provider but with cash Isas from previous tax years, you can decide whether you want to move all of it to one provider or split it across a number of different Isa accounts.

Fixed-rate bonds

Savings bonds sound serious but they're actually a simple product offered by banks and building societies. In exchange for agreeing to tie up your money for a set period of time, typically between one and five years, you'll receive a higher rate of interest than if you had opted for an instant-access savings account.

As you'd think, most savings bonds pay a fixed rate of interest, so you know exactly what you will get back when you hand your money over. However, there are also variable-rate products, such as tracker bonds, which pay the Bank of England base interest rate plus a set percentage, and inflation-linked bonds, which pay inflation plus a set percentage. Depending on the bond, interest can be paid monthly, annually or rolled up and paid on maturity.

Usually, the longer you are prepared to lock away your money, the higher the reward you will receive from the bank. Fortunately, you can begin saving with small amounts but the more you invest, the better the rate you'll get. While many providers set a minimum investment of £1,000 or more, some are far less choosy and require a deposit of just £1.

However, you can expect to pay hefty penalties for accessing your money early. Banks expect to have your money for the full period and will have invested it themselves with that in mind – so you'll usually lose some interest if you cash in your bond early.

It's worth remembering that while it's highly attractive to have a decent fixed rate that beats conventional savings accounts, if interest rates rise, then the rate on a fixed-rate bond becomes less attractive.

Don't confuse simple savings bonds with other products. Corporate bonds, for example, are issued by companies and are bought and sold via a stockbroker. As the return isn't guaranteed, your money could be at risk.

Retail bonds are a recent idea that gave companies a cheap form of finance at a time when interest rates were at all-time lows. The market for them started in February 2011, when the London Stock Exchange (LSE) launched its Order Book for Retail Bonds (Orb) but, although they are popular and can be held within an Isa, they are not the same as fixed-rate savings bonds. They are tranches of debt issued by a company, plus interest, which will be repaid at a later date. If their value falls (or the issuer goes bust), investors will not be covered by the FSCS, so you need to tread carefully.

Saving with NS&I

National Savings & Investments (NS&I) is the government's retail bank. Set up as the Post Office Savings Bank in 1861 by then Chancellor of the Exchequer William Gladstone, the aim was to offer a safe haven for savers as well as to fund public spending. These two principles remain: NS&I provides a totally secure place for people to save, backed by the government, and still provides the Exchequer with a source of funding to this day.

During the First World War, this government bank introduced savings certificates to help finance the war effort, while premium bonds were officially launched on 1 November 1956 by Harold Macmillan, then Chancellor. The first draw took place on 1 June 1957.

Over the years, NS&I has developed a range of savings and investments to meet the needs of customers, as well as the UK government's need for funding.

Because of its government backing, NS&I is arguably the safest place anyone in the UK can put their money – effectively, the government would have to go bust before you lose anything.

As well as savings certificates and premium bonds, NS&I also offers an instant-access deposit account, Isas and savings bonds.

Savings certificates are tax-free investments that pay either a fixed rate of interest or a rate linked to inflation. They can be bought by people as young as seven years old. Every so often, NS&I releases new issues of certificate, which allow you to invest between £100 and £15,000 – on top of your Isa allowance. However, at the time of writing, NS&I has withdrawn the certificates from sale and it no longer offers growth or income bonds.

Premium bonds

Premium bonds offer savers the chance of winning monthly tax-free cash prizes, from £25 to up to £1 million, in a prize draw. You can buy up to £40,000 per person, rising to £50,000 in June 2015, and you can cash in your bonds at any time.

In July 2013, NS&I lengthened the odds of any £1 premium bond winning a cash prize from 24,000 to one to 26,000 to one, while the odds of winning the £1 million monthly prize are more than 45 billion to one. However, the number of monthly £1 million premium bond prizes has doubled to two a month since August 2014.

NS&I calculates that, on average, the rate at which bondholders win prizes equates to an interest rate of 1.35% (slashed from a previous 1.5% in July 2013). However, this is most definitely an average, which means that some will earn more, while others, as it's always worth remembering, will end up with less.

This means that savers need to ask themselves whether it's worth forgoing the slightly higher interest rate they would receive from a traditional savings account in the hope of winning more in tax-free prizes offered by premium bonds. One person will, of course, win the monthly £1 million prize, too. Just don't buy and forget about them: according to NS&I, more than £44 million worth of premium bond prizes are sitting unclaimed.

Pensioner bonds

In January 2015, NS&I made available a range of new pensioner bonds – a savings bond for people aged over 65 that promise to pay better interest rates. The 65+ Guaranteed Growth Bonds (to give them their proper name) come in two versions – one paying 2.8% gross over one year, and the other paying 4% over three years. Individuals must deposit at least £500 to open an account and are limited to depositing £10,000 per bond, but they are allowed to open one of each. However, the bonds will not be available indefinitely and were expected to sell out by May 2015.

P2P lending

With savings rates poor at the time of writing, other options are emerging for savers and one of them is peer-to-peer lending – also known as social lending but often referred to more simply as P2P.

Peer-to-peer lending websites bring together borrowers in need of loans with savers who have money to lend, providing a viable alternative to a traditional bank. By cutting out the middleman, borrowers get a competitive rate on their loans and lenders get a better return on their money.

You can lend to individuals needing money for cars, home improvements and so on through sites such as Zopa, RateSetter and Lending Works, or you can even help fund small- to medium-sized start-up companies and businesses though players such as Funding Circle and Thin Cats.

According to estimates from innovation charity Nesta, £547 million was lent through P2P firms such as Zopa and RateSetter – the current market leaders – in 2014, with an average loan size of almost £5,500.

P2P is, then, an antidote to the stuffy world of high street banking. By cutting out all the expensive infrastructure that the likes of Barclays and HSBC have to deal with – a huge network of branches, thousands of staff, vast administration teams and so on – internet-based social lenders are able to operate quickly and cheaply.

P2P has been around for a decade now – Zopa, the pioneer of social lending, launched in 2005. But until recently it has been considered a niche option. However, the sector is now regulated by the Financial Conduct Authority and the government has said it will allow lenders to hold P2P savings in an Isa (this is currently being consulted on and an announcement is expected in the summer of 2015), meaning P2P is now making its way into the mainstream.

The returns offered are currently better than the interest rate on bank savings accounts. Zopa offers lenders a rate of 5.1% on loans of up to three or five years; while RateSetter offers a return of 6% on its five-year deal (both before tax).

Accounts tend to be flexible, allowing you to manage your investment as you wish. If income is your priority, you can take your capital and interest repayments each month to top up your income. Or if you have no immediate need for the money, you can reinvest it in new loans. RateSetter takes it a step further and allows you to take your interest and reinvest your capital.

Anyone over the age of 18 can lend (that is, save) with RateSetter or Zopa and you can lend as little as £10. RateSetter says someone lending £10,000 via the RateSetter rolling monthly access account would have earned 72% more in interest (£440) than someone saving via the NS&I one-year bond over the same period.

However, P2P lending is far from risk-free. While it is to become eligible for inclusion inside an Isa wrapper and is now regulated by the FCA, lenders' deposits are not protected by the Financial Services Compensation Scheme. That said, the likes of Zopa and RateSetter have introduced their own protections.

RateSetter, for example, operates a 'Provision Fund' that allows for a lender to be repaid their capital and interest if borrowers miss a payment (it will lend your money to a single borrower, unlike Zopa which splits lenders' money across a range of borrowers). But it is by no means a guarantee – if RateSetter went bust, for example, your money would be at risk. That said, Zopa and RateSetter both operate stringent credit checks before taking on borrowers too and, to date, no lender has lost their capital with either of the two industry leaders.

Still, independent financial advisers may acknowledge the sector's popularity but seem to be wary of recommending it to their clients, perhaps because it's only been regulated since April 2014.

Finally, remember that P2P lending is very different from the other areas of crowdfunding. For example, equity crowdfunding is where people invest money in small business ventures, usually in return for an equity stake in the business or for a promised return when the business turns a profit – turning lenders into mini dragons à la *Dragons' Den*. Equity crowdfunding is far higher risk than P2P lending, as shares in any business can rise and fall in value, while small businesses and start-up firms are riskier still because so many go bust.

'Sweep' to save

Sweeping extra cash directly from your current account to your savings account will help you to save effectively. You won't miss the money after a while and it means you can continue saving without interruption. You can set this up automatically so that at the end of each month your bank will take whatever is left above a certain limit and transfer it into your savings account. If you don't want this kind of automatic sweep, you could simply set up a monthly standing order to a savings account of your choice for a fixed amount each month, then make a note to check whether you had more left than you thought and move that across manually.

Don't be afraid to switch

Despite the low rates currently being offered to savers, it is important to get into the habit of checking the interest you're getting from your bank, as it could cost you.

Savingschampion.co.uk has warned that a saver with £50,000 in an easy-access savings account could be losing out on £800 a year by placing their money in a poor-paying account.

Yet many consumers are guilty of inertia when it comes to their accounts, or are simply unaware that an account that paid a decent rate when they opened it years ago is now an underperformer. This is particularly the case with accounts that come with bonuses. Banks and building societies hope you have forgotten all about it when the bonus deal expires and you are reverted to a poor standard rate.

The same is true with fixed-rate bonds, so when the product matures, ditch and switch. Switching is one of the easiest ways of getting the best deals from bank accounts – loyalty is rarely rewarded.

PART 3:
Get Organised

Getting married

You're getting married? Congratulations! When is the big day? Where's it going to be? Have you thought about colour schemes? Will you have a theme?

It's easy to get carried away but before you get wedding fever there's something a little less romantic you need to do first: work out how much you can afford to spend on it all.

A survey by *Brides Magazine* in November 2014 put the average cost of a UK wedding at £19,363. Excluding the honeymoon, the three biggest expenses were the reception venue at £4,189, the catering at £3,063 and the wedding ceremony venue at £2,223.

Average wedding costs

ITEM	COST
Wedding venue	£2,223
Reception venue	£4,189
Catering	£3,063
Photography/video	£1,399
Flowers	£560
Cake	£296
Entertainment	£682
Dress	£1,340
Shoes	£107
Stationery	£240
Headdress/veil	£108
Groom's outfit	£313
Ushers' outfits	£465
Wedding rings	£647
Honeymoon	£3,931
Total	£19,363
Source: Brides Magazine, *average reader spend, November 2014*	

That almost £20,000 total is serious money, whether you'll be footing the bill yourself or getting help from your parents or others. But there are plenty of ways to help cut the cost. Here are three to get you started.

1. **Pick your date carefully.** If you get married out of peak season, which runs from May to September and then hots up again during December, not only will you have more flexibility on dates but you could also bag yourself a few bargains as lots of venues and wedding suppliers will offer discounts at this time. The day of the week you pick can also have a bearing on the cost, as wedding venues and suppliers are also more likely to offer discounts for bookings between Monday and Thursday. Of course, getting married on a weekday could make it harder for your guests to attend but if you're planning a small wedding with your closest friends and family, you could save yourself a lot of money. And if you want to get married quickly, you could also save by booking a last-minute wedding package.

2. **Make the most of sales and wedding fairs**. Keep an eye out for sales at wedding dress shops – usually advertised as 'designer days' – as well as on the rest of the high street and you'll be able to save yourself money on everything from outfits to decorations. Similarly, visiting wedding fairs at popular venues not only allows you to get an idea of how the venue may be dressed on your big day but also local suppliers attend to exhibit their services and many will offer discounts if you book there and then.

3. **Do it yourself.** There are so many little jobs involved in planning a traditional wedding and, while it's tempting to throw money at the situation to save yourself time and hassle, there are plenty of things you can do yourself simply and inexpensively. For instance, why spend money on buying favours when there are hundreds of things you could make at home? Biscuits and jam go down a storm. Of course, there will be a cost for ingredients and packaging but chances are you'll save yourself money compared to buying the finished article from somewhere else.

There are things you can do that won't cost you a penny, too. For example, why waste money on buying or printing 'save the date' cards, when you could email your guests? OK, this might not sound very romantic but you could create a glamorous, personalised design on your computer, save it as a PDF and then email everyone the attachment. That way, you can inject bags of personality at no cost at all. You can then put the money you'll save towards the invitations themselves – unless the email bug takes hold and you go for e-invites.

Ways to pay

Once you've got an idea of how much it will cost, you'll need to consider how you plan to pay for your wedding.

The first cost you are likely to encounter will be the deposit for the venue, often around a third of the overall price upfront. Other supplier deposits will soon follow – namely, for your photographer, florist, entertainment and the all-important wedding dress.

Of course, paying for all this with cash from savings would be great and, as we say in the Save Money section, saving rather than borrowing remains the ideal. However, it's also true that many newly engaged couples often find themselves about to buy their first home too, so any spare cash is usually tied up in saving a deposit for a mortgage. However, there are some alternative ways to finance your wedding and spread the costs, such as a credit card that charges 0% interest on purchases, or a personal loan.

As a rule of thumb, a credit card can be a good idea for some of your smaller payments such as outfits, invitations, flowers and deposits, while a personal loan can be sensible for the more expensive parts of your spend. This is because it's generally possible to borrow a larger sum of money through a personal loan than the limit a credit-card provider will set.

If you go for a 0% purchase credit card, as long as you pay the minimum amount off each month, you can spread your payments over a number of months depending on the card you take out. Credit card deals change all the time and at the time of writing the longest 0% offer was for 20 months.

Alternatively, if you already have a balance on another credit card that no longer offers you 0% interest on your purchases, you could move your balance to a balance-transfer credit card and pay 0% on it for more than two years in some cases. You'll normally have to pay a fee of up to 3% of your balance for the convenience but a balance-transfer card can be a good way to stagger your wedding spend over a longer period.

As well as being able to spread the cost, another important advantage of using a credit card for your wedding spending is that your purchases are protected by Section 75 of the Consumer Credit Act 1974. This means that if anything goes wrong with a supplier – if it goes bust or fails to provide the goods or services you paid for, you'll be able to get your money back on purchases of between £100 and £30,000.

However, bear in mind that some suppliers may charge you a fee for paying by credit card (typically 2% or 3%), so always check in advance and weigh up the pros and cons of paying by card.

Wedding insurance

Is it worth insuring your wedding? The answer depends on whether you are concerned about unforeseen circumstances jeopardising your big day.

If so, comprehensive wedding insurance policies provide cover for cancellation. This means that should a member of the bridal party fall seriously ill, or should something happen to your venue, such as a fire, and you are unable to go ahead with your wedding as planned, your money will be protected.

Each policy differs as to how much it will pay out, and the amount of cover you require will affect the price of your premium. A comprehensive policy with cancellation cover of £20,000 costs around £60.

Thankfully, the chances of having to cancel a wedding outright are slim but rearrangement is more likely and so it's a good idea to make sure your policy also covers this.

If you do decide to go for wedding insurance, there are a few exclusions to be aware of. For example, cancellation cover does not apply to cold feet; it covers only cancellation due to 'circumstances beyond your control', so if the bride or groom decides to jilt the other at the altar it could prove to be financially, as well as emotionally, devastating.

Also, some policies won't cover deposits already paid to suppliers before your wedding insurance was taken out. Others won't pay out for damage caused by anyone under the influence of alcohol. However, your venue's public liability insurance – cover for injury or damage caused by you or your wedding guests – will usually pay out regardless of alcohol consumption. That said, your venue may be less than keen to claim on its own insurance and could seek to recover any losses from you.

So always read the small print of your insurance policy so that you understand all the terms and conditions carefully before signing up.

Remember, insurance is typically only necessary if you can't afford to replace the cost of what you're insuring. So, before you take out a wedding insurance policy, break down your budget and work out how much cover you would need realistically for each area of spend. For example, there's no point paying to be covered for £5,000 worth of photography if your photographer will charge you only £1,000.

Currently, none of the big comparison sites cover wedding insurance but there is a smaller site trying to fill the void: **compareweddinginsurance.org.uk** isn't a bad place to start looking for a policy. All companies listed on the site are regulated by the Financial Ombudsman Service (FOS) and are protected by the Financial Services Compensation Scheme (FSCS).

Pre-nups

On getting married, both assets and liabilities become shared. So while it might be great to become a co-owner of a home, finding that your credit rating has been dented by your spouse's irresponsible attitude to debt – or worse still, finding out that a bailiff might come after your belongings to pay off your spouse's debt – could come as an unwelcome wedding gift.

Before walking down the aisle, some couples choose to sign a pre-nuptial agreement (commonly known as a 'pre-nup') setting out what will happen in relation to their financial affairs in the event of a divorce. Couples often see them as a form of insurance, whereby you spend a lesser sum of money upfront to avoid paying out a lot more should the marriage come to an end.

It is important to note that pre-nups are not legally binding in England, Wales and Northern Ireland, although they are legally binding in Scotland – a February 2014 report by the Law Commission recommended that pre-nups do become enshrined in law in the UK. Until then, a court may still take it into consideration when assessing the financial entitlement of each party, so long as it believes the contract was entered into willingly and is not 'manifestly unfair' to either party.

Pre-nups are not just for Hollywood A-listers. They are drawn up by lots of different people, including those entering second marriages who want to protect any previously acquired wealth for children from a prior marriage. Alternatively, they might be taken out by couples where only one partner has substantial personal wealth, or those who want to ringfence an inheritance they expect to receive.

A properly drawn-up pre-nup doesn't come cheap (up to £3,000 in London) but it can result in real savings if it later helps to reduce expensive legal costs during the divorce process.

The financial implications of marriage

- Marriage will automatically revoke any existing will. To avoid this, a new will needs to be made in advance of marriage, should be stated "in contemplation of marriage" and include a statement that such marriage should not revoke the will.

- Married couples and civil partners who pay different levels of tax are able to reduce their capital gains tax (CGT) bills. Basic-rate taxpayers have to pay CGT at 18%, whereas a higher-rate payer does so at 28%. So where capital gains exceed the annual CGT exemption (£11,100 per person in the 2015/16 tax year), a couple can save money on their CGT bill by transferring ownership of an asset to the spouse paying the lower rate thus reducing their overall tax liability (although this may not remove the whole of the higher rate liability; for example, if total income exceeds the higher rate income tax threshold).

- Anything left to a spouse or civil partner is exempt from inheritance tax (IHT). The survivor is allowed to 'inherit' any unused part of their spouse's nil-rate band (what they are allowed to receive before they have to pay tax) – £325,000 in the 2015/16 tax year. At the current rate, this means that up to £650,000 can then be passed on to children on the death of the second spouse. In comparison, unmarried partners can pass assets only up to the nil-rate band of £325,000 without having to pay IHT, which kicks in at 40% on estates worth more than £325,000. See page 151 for more on IHT.

- Since 6 April 2015, married spouses can transfer up to £1,060 of their unused income tax personal allowance (which is £10,600 in the 2015/16 tax year) to their spouse, which Prime Minister David Cameron says could bring about a saving of £200 a year. Non-working spouses, or ones who haven't used up their full personal tax allowance, will be able to transfer £1,060 to their spouse as long as that person is a basic-rate taxpayer (earning less than £42,700 a year). Couples must apply online to receive the benefit by the summer of 2016.

- Married couples where either spouse was born before 6 April 1935 may qualify for Married Couple's Allowance, a tax relief from the government that could have saved them between £314 and £816.50 in the 2014/15 tax year.

Having a child

Raising a child will change your life in all sorts of ways – most of them wonderful, of course – but one factor parents can underestimate is the effect it will have on their finances. While babies are expensive in their own right, the loss of one partner's salary when caring for the child – or costly nursery fees if both partners continue working – can have a serious impact.

In 2014, it cost £11,224 on average to raise a child in their first year, according to research from insurance company LV=, which has been tracking the cost for the past 11 years. The annual cost rises to £15,271 between the ages of one and four, before falling to £12,118 a year between the ages of five and 10. It then dips slightly again to £7,869 between ages 11 and 17. But between the ages of 18 and 21, children cost £17,794 every year.

So based on the 2014 figures, raising a child to the age of 21 could cost parents £229,251.

As the following table shows, childcare accounts for a significant amount of the overall cost. The average nursery charge in Britain for a child under the age of two is £115.45 a week for a part-time place (25 hours) in 2015, or more than £6,000 a year, according to the Family and Childcare Trust (formerly the Daycare Trust). The cost of full-time care rises to £212.09 a week.

Average childminder costs for under-twos stood at £104.06, based on 25 hours of care a week, and £196.55 for 50 hours.

Meanwhile, for school-age children, 15 hours at an after-school club costs £48.18, and the Family and Childcare Trust says a typical working family with one child in part-time nursery care and one child in an after-school club will pay almost £8,000 a year for care.

With such sizeable sums involved, it's best to start planning your family finances as soon as possible.

COST BREAKDOWN OF RAISING A CHILD TO THE AGE OF 21	
CATEGORY	COST
Education	£74,319
Childcare and babysitting	£67,586
Food	£19,517
Clothing	£10,942
Holidays	£16,675
Hobbies and toys	£9,377
Leisure and recreation	£7,486
Pocket money	£4,603
Furniture	£3,434
Personal	£1,146
Other	£14,167
Total	£229,251

Source: LV=

Don't worry, we're not going to teach you about conception – we figure that if you're reading a guide to personal finance, you're savvy enough to know how that works already. Instead, here's our list of what you need to look at far in advance of the birth of your baby.

First things first: work out what your rights to maternity leave are and how much you will earn while you are off work.

Maternity leave and pay

All new mothers are entitled to take Statutory Maternity Leave for up to a year. It doesn't matter how long you've been with your employer, how many hours you work or how much you get paid.

Every woman has different circumstances and you don't have to take the full 52 weeks off but you must take two weeks' leave after your baby is born (or four weeks if you work in a factory).

Usually, the earliest maternity leave can start is 11 weeks before the expected week of childbirth. But should your bundle of joy make an early appearance, leave will start the day after the birth. Or should you fall ill with a pregnancy-related condition in the four weeks before your due date and be unable to work, your maternity leave will kick in automatically – as will Statutory Maternity Pay (SMP).

If you decide to take the full year off work, you will have six months (26 weeks) of Ordinary Maternity Leave. If you return to work during this period, you have the right to return to exactly the same job that you had before you left. But after those six months, you can choose to take a further 26 weeks of Additional Maternity Leave. If you are taking more than six months' leave, you have a right to return to the same job – unless it is no longer available. Should that be the case, you must be given a similar job with the same pay and conditions.

You must also give your employer notice at least 15 weeks before your due date, telling them when your child is due and when you want to start your maternity leave. You can do this verbally, but your employer can ask for it in writing, too.

How much is maternity pay?

Statutory Maternity Pay (SMP) – the minimum amount you must receive by law – is paid for up to 39 weeks. If you are an employee, you are entitled to get 90% of your average weekly earnings (before tax) for the first six weeks of your maternity leave, followed by £139.58 or 90% of your average weekly earnings (whichever is lower) for the next 33 weeks. It is paid by your employer in the same way as your wages, be that monthly or weekly, and tax and National Insurance will be deducted.

On the average female UK salary in 2014 of £23,889, total SMP over the 39-week period (at the then rate) worked out at £7,087. She would have earned £17,916 before tax had she been working normally, meaning she lost £10,829 or 60% of her gross income while on maternity leave.

After taxes, this represents a loss in take-home pay of around £7,500. As salary rises, so does the proportion lost – 65% of gross for someone earning £30,000, 70% at £40,000 and 74% at £50,000. While she may get some of her tax back once her earnings start to dip, the impact of lost earnings remains significant.

To be eligible for SMP, you must have been working for your employer continuously for at least 26 weeks up to the 15th week before your baby is due. This is commonly known as the 'qualifying week'. There is also a minimum earnings threshold and you must earn on average, at least £111 a week.

The government has a maternity pay calculator you can tap your details into at **gov.uk/calculate-your-maternity-pay** so you can find out exactly what you will receive after you have had your baby. If you experience any difficulties with your employer concerning your maternity leave or pay, you can contact the government's Statutory Payment Disputes Team on 0300 056 0630.

Shared parental leave

Parents of babies due or children matched or placed for adoption on or after 5 April 2015 can share up to 50 weeks of paternity leave, and 37 weeks of statutory maternity pay, between them. Mums must still take two weeks off after the birth.

How does maternity leave affect your pension?

If you contribute to a workplace pension scheme, you and your employer will both continue to make pension contributions as long as you are getting paid during your maternity leave. However, if you extend your maternity leave beyond a year and take this time unpaid, while you may usually be able to make contributions should you wish to, you don't have to and neither does your employer – unless your contract of employment says otherwise.

Nearly a third of new mums go into debt after taking maternity leave. Figures from comparison website uSwitch reveal that 28% end up in the red, with an average debt of £2,500, and that 10% of those who return to work cut short their time off to ease the financial burden.

State help: Child Benefit

Child Benefit is paid straight into your bank account every four weeks, tax-free. It is paid at a rate of £20.70 a week for the first child and £13.70 a week for each additional child.

Child Benefit stops when your child reaches age 16, although it can be paid until they reach 20 years of age if they are in education or training that qualifies for Child Benefit.

All parents used to qualify for Child Benefit but in January 2013 it was reduced for households in which the breadwinner earns £50,000 or more - even if that person isn't the parent (for example, a step-parent or co-habiting partner of the parent). This reduction works out at 1% of Child Benefit for every £100 the main breadwinner earns above £50,000. For those earning £60,000 and above, no Child Benefit is paid at all. HM Revenue & Customs estimates more than one million families have lost some or all of their Child Benefit since the beginning of 2013.

In a weird quirk to the system, households in which only one person works and earns more than £60,000 will see their benefit taken away completely, while a household made up of two people working and earning just shy of £50,000 each - so almost £100,000 between them - will keep the full benefit.

In a second quirk, while higher earners lose some or all of the benefit, unless they opt out of the Child Benefit scheme, they continue to receive the payments and then have to repay the money by completing a self-assessment tax return at the end of the relevant tax year, through the 'High Income Charge'. Failure to do so can result in penalty fees being charged.

Individuals who earn £50,000 or more could use salary sacrifice to effectively reduce their income in order to keep some or all of their Child Benefit.

Childcare vouchers

Childcare vouchers are the most obvious form of salary sacrifice to look into. Working parents can buy vouchers from their employers and use them to pay for nannies, nurseries, childminders and after-school clubs for children up to the age of 15 (until 1 September following their 15th birthday) or 16 (until 1 September following their 16th birthday) if they are disabled.

Both parents are able to buy them out of gross income (before tax has been deducted), making them a tax-efficient option. Basic-rate taxpayers are allowed to buy up to £55 worth of vouchers a week, while higher-rate payers are able to buy only £28 of vouchers and additional-rate payers £25 a week.

Because you won't pay tax or National Insurance on childcare vouchers, families paying tax at the basic rate can save up to £933 a year if one parent buys them, or £1,866 if both of them do. Meanwhile, higher-rate and additional-rate taxpayers can save up to £623 each, or £1,246 if both parents work and buy vouchers.

Working parents can buy the vouchers (either paper vouchers or an online version) through their employer's own scheme or one it has signed up to through a childcare voucher provider. Employers aren't obliged to offer a scheme and if yours doesn't, it's always worth asking it to consider doing so. Employers could save up to £400 a year per employee thanks to reduced National Insurance contributions.

If you are expecting your first child, you are not allowed to buy any vouchers until the baby is born but with subsequent children, you can stock up while pregnant. An employer is obliged to continue giving you the vouchers during maternity leave and to meet the cost if your pay ends up below the statutory minimum.

There are some exclusions. For example, only working parents earning less than £150,000 a year each, who are not receiving tax credits or who are not already part of an employer childcare scheme, are allowed to buy the vouchers. Additionally, self-employed parents are not eligible for the scheme but company directors are.

However, there are drawbacks to taking childcare vouchers. Since voucher-buyers pay less tax and National Insurance, any state benefits linked to these contributions can be affected, including Statutory Maternity Pay and Statutory Sick Pay.

From autumn 2015, the government plans to introduce a new Tax-Free Childcare Scheme that won't be limited to employers, so more families can benefit, including the self-employed and carers. Under the proposals, parents will set up an account with NS&I and save money towards the cost of childcare. They'll be able to claim back tax relief at 20% out of the £10,000 the government estimates the average annual cost of a childcare place to be. And that clawback is per child under the age of 12 (or 16, in the case of disabled children).

Only families with both parents working (including on a self-employed basis), but earning less than £150,000 each, will be able to join the scheme.

Parents who join a childcare voucher scheme before the introduction of the Tax-Free Childcare Scheme will be able to continue to use childcare vouchers or switch to the new scheme. However, childcare vouchers will cease to be available to new parents after the introduction of the Tax-Free Childcare Scheme.

Whether your family will be better off with the old or new scheme will depend on your circumstances, such as how much you spend on childcare, how many children you have and whether one or both parents work.

Lots of families are entitled to Child Tax Credits or the childcare element of the Working Tax Credit to help pay some of their childcare costs while they are working.

Child Tax Credits

You'll get a basic amount of up to £545 a year for each child that qualifies, along with extra 'elements' of up to £2,780 a year for each child (rising to £3,140 if the child is disabled and a further £1,275 a year if that child is severely disabled).

To qualify, each child you're responsible for must be under 16 or under 20 and in approved education or training. But how much you get depends on your circumstances and only one household can get Child Tax Credit for a child.

Childcare element of the Working Tax Credit

You could get up to £175 a week for one child and up to £300 a week for two children or more but this increases according to your circumstances – for example, if your child is disabled. The maximum proportion of eligible childcare costs that will be covered is 70%.

As a rough guide, if you have one child and the annual household income is below £26,000, you'll likely qualify. However, it can be higher if you pay for approved childcare.

Also bear in mind that parents who are entitled to the childcare element of the Working Tax Credit could lose out if they choose childcare vouchers instead. The rules are very complicated so to find specific information relevant to your personal situation, call the government's Tax Credit Helpline on 0345 300 3900. You can also get an idea of what childcare support you might be entitled to by using HM Revenue & Customs' online childcare calculator at **hmrc.gov.uk/calcs/ccin.htm**.

The real cost of having a baby

Having your first child is a daunting experience, not least because of the effect it will have on your finances. If you want to know what you can expect while you're expecting, here's a guide to the likely costs you'll incur throughout your journey to becoming a parent.

Pregnancy

Pregnancy tests: There's a huge range of tests available from chemists and supermarkets – not to mention online retailers. Some of the most popular brands, including Clearblue and First Response, have tests priced from around £8.50. The results are typically displayed as a simple cross for positive and single line for negative.

Moving up the price scale are digital tests that display results on a screen showing a 'pregnant' or 'not pregnant' result. Some models also give an indication of how far along a pregnancy may be. The price for these tests is closer to £12 but they usually come in a pack of two.

Whichever type of test you're looking for, shopping around online will save you money. Amazon sells packs of 15 very basic paper strip tests for just £2.80 with free delivery. But if bargain basement isn't what you're after, you can still save on well-known makes. For example, Boots sells a pack of 'Clearblue Pregnancy Test – 3 tests' for £12.99 in its stores and charges an extra £2.95 for deliveries under £45 if you buy items online. However, a quick Google search reveals that the same tests can be bought on eBay for £10.49 with free postage.

Scans and photos: During your pregnancy, you will have two 2D ultrasound scans provided for free as standard by the NHS at 12 and 20 weeks, with the latter scan offering to identify the gender of your baby – though not with 100% certainty. If you want to take away a photo, hospitals usually let you do so in return for a £2 donation. Private 3D and 4D scans are also available and these can give you a much more detailed look at your baby and the ability to find out what gender it is.

Prices vary significantly. Some companies include a couple of printed photos in their scan package deals, others include a range of images and/or videos on CD Roms/DVDs. For example, Baby Scanning, which runs clinics in Scotland, has a range of packages available with a discounted gender scan deal advertised on its website in late January for £37. The scan can be carried out from 16 weeks and the appointment lasts for up to ten minutes. No images are supplied. For £59, the 3D Baby Scans package includes a 15-minute appointment with a CD Rom of up to ten still 3D scan images and two A4-sized 3D scan pictures to take home. It's also possible to find out the baby's gender.

NCT classes: Your GP will often recommend you attend an antenatal course to help you prepare for birth and parenthood. A lot of courses across the UK are run by the NCT charity, formerly called the National Childbirth Trust. However, despite being a charity, parents have to pay for classes, although discounts of up to 90% are offered to those on low incomes and there is an option to pay in instalments. The NCT says these discounts mean classes can cost as little as £7 in some cases. For everyone else, they cost a lot more.

Prices are based on where you live (three price bands apply: A, the cheapest; B; and C, the London band and most expensive), the number of teaching hours and whether you attend alone or take a partner along with you.

There are two antenatal courses to choose from – the Essentials course, or the Signature.

NCT Essentials courses start at £70 and include six two-hour sessions with fixed content and structure. Five of those sessions take place during pregnancy and the last one after the baby arrives, at a 'postnatal reunion'. Prices start at £70 for mums attending alone and who live in a 'Band A' postcode, but this rises to £90 in Band B and £115 in Band C (the London price band). If mum wants to take a partner with her, the course costs jump to £120, £150 and £190 respectively, though bear in mind one of the sessions will be a breastfeeding class attended only by prospective mums.

The Signature antenatal course is a bit trickier when it comes to pricing as "every course is tailored to the needs of the small group taking part", says the NCT. Each course is flexible, meaning the number of hours they take up can vary but they typically range from 14 to 21 hours. The price per hour in Band A is currently £10, rising to £12.80 in Band B and £16.70 in Band C.

To find specific prices of different courses running in your area, visit **nct.org.uk/courses/course-prices** and enter your postcode and your baby's due date as some courses are designed for different stages of your pregnancy. You can also find loads of free information on the site about pregnancy, birth and the first 1,000 days as a new parent.

Free antenatal courses are available from Sure Start Children's Centre, which are open to all parents. Find your nearest centre at **gov.uk/find-sure-start-childrens-centre**.

The kit you'll need

Before we get started with the shopping list, bear in mind that there is a massive range of options available and prices vary dramatically. The products and prices given here are examples of popular brands and how much they typically cost from major retailers.

Hospital bag

A lot of the items the NHS recommends you pack, you're likely to already have at home (such as loose fitting clothes – particularly loose vests – and toiletries). But there are a few bits you'll probably need to buy, including baby clothes (and a hat), a shawl, nappies and a nursing bra. Mothercare sells starter packs of three plain white bodysuits (babygrows without the legs) for £5, and a two pack of 'Oatmeal Printed and Stripy Hats' (perfect if you don't know the sex of your baby) also for £5. Shawls start at £10 on its website.

As for maternity/nursing bras, M&S sells two packs in a variety of styles and colours all for £29.50, while individual bras are available from John Lewis starting at £16.50. Last but by no means least, while nappies will cost you a small fortune over the next couple of years, for your first purchase you won't have to dig too deep. While smaller packs are available, a 'value pack' of 45 Pampers New Baby Size 1 (Newborn) Nappies cost £6.99 from Superdrug, that's 15.5p per nappy. Buy a jumbo pack of 72 and the price per nappy falls quite a bit. Online retailer Playten is selling them for £9 (free delivery) – just 12.5p per nappy. And by the way, you'll probably get through ten a day to begin with!

Join the club

Almost every retailer that sells baby products has clubs that parents can join in order to receive freebies, discounts vouchers and product samples. Boots, for example, offers double Advantage Card points on baby products (10 points for every £1 you spend – excluding stage one formula milk), free gifts such as Johnson's baby shampoo, and a changing bag.

Many clubs, such as Asda's Baby & Toddler Club, will keep you informed by email when the retailer holds a major baby event in-store, where you can pick up the likes of nappies at heavily discounted prices.

If you plan to join all of the clubs, you'll end up with a purse or wallet-full of handy discount vouchers that means you'll rarely pay full price for the essentials (stage one formula milk aside). However, it's worth creating a separate email address at which you can direct all your baby club emails, to save them overloading your main inbox.

Formula

If you don't plan to breastfeed, or will be combination feeding, you will need to buy baby formula (known as stage one formula milk) – and a lot of it. The law dictates that no discounts can be offered, so while there are differences in prices between makes, there are no significant savings to be made whether you buy in store or online. You won't earn supermarket loyalty card points either.

A quick scan for prices of Aptamil First Infant Milk Powder from Birth Onwards Stage 1 (900g) at **mysupermarket.co.uk** shows a difference of just a penny across the big four chains, with Asda, Morrisons and Sainsbury's selling it for £9.99 and Tesco a penny more at £10. So how long will that last your baby? Well, it all depends on how much and how often they eat but here's a rough calculation. Each scoop contains 4 grams so the 900 gram tin has 225 recommended servings. If your baby takes around 30 ounces of formula a day, the tin will last around a week.

Getting home

On leaving the hospital, you'll need a car seat. And while price is an important consideration, all that really matters is safety. Buying secondhand really isn't a good idea as you won't know if its safety features have been compromised by an accident or simply heavy usage. It's also vital to buy a model that is compatible with your car, and to have it properly fitted.

When you start shopping for a seat, you can find lots of recommendations online from parent and consumer groups and these can be useful in pointing you in the right direction.

Experts recommend the first car seat you buy should be 'a rear-facing infant carrier', which should fit your child throughout their first year until they weigh around 13kg. The Concord Air Group 0+ fared well in a review of carseats by the *Independent* newspaper. The review said: "It has great front and side impact protection and good head support, and is a doddle to install. We also found it lighter to carry than a lot on the market." Argos sells it in-store for £109.99 and delivery costs £3.95. The Graco Snugsafe also did well in the review and was noted for being a good lightweight option. It's on sale at **pramcentre.co.uk** for £84.99 with free delivery.

When buying a car seat, product descriptions will usually include mention of whether it can be used with or without an isofix base. This is a type of fitting that makes installation easier to fit the seat correctly. New cars often include this as standard but an isofix base can be bought separately – at a cost of around £100 – for use in any car. Don't feel pressured into splashing out on the fitting aid though. Carseats that are solely secured by traditional seatbelts are perfectly safe.

It's also worth noting that some car seats are designed to fit into a pram chassis, so you can purchase a combination of car seat, pram and chassis that will suit your baby for walks as well as driving in the car. (There's more on prams on page 123.) And one final point about car seats: consumer group Which? publishes a list of best-buy car seats each year that its members can download from the website. This list is widely considered to be the industry standard. While membership costs £10.95 a month, you can sign up for a trial for £1 to gain access to the list. Just make sure you cancel your membership at the end of the trial or you'll be charged the full monthly fee.

For the first several months of your baby's life, you may find your new arrival sharing your bedroom. At this time, they usually sleep in a Moses basket rather than a cot. They're fairly inexpensive, with prices for the basket starting from £35 at John Lewis and Mothercare, while the stands you'll also need start at £30 and £14.99 respectively.

Most of the rest of the kit you'll need revolves around feeding, changing and bathing. While formula prices are outlined above, other things you'll need for feeding include bottles and possibly a bottle steriliser. Bottles can be very cheap. Boots sells its Standard Necked Baby Feeding Bottle – 250ml for just 18p each or a five-pack of Tommee Tippee Steri-bottle® 250ml for £4.49. Once you decide which brand to go for, it's worth noting that that range will also usually have compatible teats, sterilisers and other accessories.

As for sterilisers, there's a huge range available at prices from £12 to £60. The lower prices are for compact sets you can fit in the microwave such as the Philips Avent SCF281/02 Microwave Steam Steriliser, which cleans up to four Avent bottles or two breast pumps per time and costs around £12. At the other end of the price scale, you'll find models such as the Avent 3-in-1 Electric Steam Steriliser (£60), which cleans teats, bottles (up to six) and pumps.

If you are on a budget, you can also simply buy a large sealable Tupperware box and some Milton tablets for sterilising – search online for how to do it.

Finally, there are loads of changing mats and baby baths to choose from, too, and they are largely inexpensive. They can be easily bought for less than £10 each.

Out and about

When you're on the move, you'll probably need a pram – or travel system, as they are more often known as these days. They can be very expensive – some cost more than a car!

The most expensive John Lewis sells is the iCandy Peach Blossom 3 Twin Pushchair with Chrome Chassis and Marshmallow Hood at an eye-watering £1,180.00. At Mothercare, travel system prices start at £199 for the Xpedior 4 Wheel Pram & Pushchair Travel System, which includes a carseat.

A good tip when shopping for your first pram is to buy it as close to the birth as possible. If you buy too far in advance you won't have full use of the warranty if you spot any problems when you're finally ready to get out of the house.

And remember, there's a very healthy secondhand market for higher-end makes such as Bugaboo so check websites such as Gumtree and eBay for bargains.

Children's savings

As your children grow, you will have to find the money for short-term spending needs – such as toys, clothes, school trips and hobbies. While regularly saving each month in an easy-access savings account will help you build up a pot you can dip into as and when these costs arise, this type of savings account usually pays a low rate of interest (see more on saving from page 89). It won't really help you for longer-term goals.

If you want to start building a more significant fund to help pay for your child's first car, to put them through university, or even to help them buy their first home, there are some much more suitable savings options available.

With around 18 years until your child is likely to need a serious cash injection, you can afford to take a little more risk with the money they put away in the hope of securing higher returns. Historically, stock market investments deliver better returns than cash but, of course, the value of any investment can fall as well as rise.

Whichever you go for, the secret to success is to get started early.

Junior Isas

An easy and tax-efficient way to invest in stocks and shares for children is through a Junior individual savings account (Jisa). These are long-term savings accounts for children. Parents, friends and family are able to pay in a total of £4,080 a year in the 2015/16 tax year. Accounts can be opened for children under 16 (16- and 17-year-olds are able to open Jisas themselves) who don't already have a Child Trust Fund. The money can't be accessed until they turn 18, at which point the money becomes theirs to do with as they please.

Money can be held in cash or stocks and shares. With a stocks-and-shares Isa, there is more potential for the money to make greater returns over the long term, as the money will be invested in the stock market. You won't pay tax on any capital growth or dividends received (although the investment funds do).

An added benefit of Jisas is that any interest earned is treated as the child's, so parents can shield some money for their kids away from taxation. With other children's savings and investments, if interest or income earned exceeds £100 in any tax year, the money can be taxed as if it were the parents'.

Child Trust Fund

The Child Trust Fund (CTF) was the precursor to the Junior Isa and was available from the government to all children born between 1 September 2002 and 2 January 2011. An account was automatically opened by HM Revenue & Customs with a £250 free gift for each child. Three types of account were available: a stakeholder, share or savings account.

With the stakeholder and share accounts, money was invested in a number of stock market-listed companies, meaning the value of the CTF pot could go up or down. In the savings-account version, the money was secure and earned interest.

If your child has a CTF, the limit you are able to deposit in the 2015/16 tax year is £4,080. Like Jisas, the money belongs to the child and can't be taken out until they're 18.

From April 2015, parents with a CTF for their children have been able to transfer them into Jisas to take advantage of better interest rates. Before this was allowed, because CTFs hadn't been available to new customers for several years, banks and building societies had no incentive to offer attractive rates to savers and, as a result, the rates available on CTF accounts were much less competitive than their Jisa peers.

Investment trusts

This type of collective investment can be opened on behalf of a child and 'designated' with their name or initials. This means parents keep control of the money and can access it but the money is meant for the child. Parents can transfer it into their child's name once they turn 18 or keep it in their own name.

In a nutshell, investment trusts are companies that buy and sell shares in other companies or assets to make a profit. They are professionally managed and diversified across lots of different companies and industries. If the investment trust is held in an Isa, you don't have to pay income or capital gains tax on any money you make from it.

You can invest regularly on a monthly basis – from £25 in many cases – or you can open a trust with a lump sum, typically of at least £250. They are flexible investments and you can stop, start or change your payments at any time.

Investment trusts have competitive charges and have performed well over the long term.

For more information on investment trusts, visit the Association of Investment Companies' website at **theaic.co.uk**. There's also more on them on page 19.

Children's pensions

If you have an even longer-term goal for helping your children financially rather than helping them pay for university or a wedding, it's also possible to set up a pension for them.

In the 2015/16 tax year, you can pay in up to £2,880 a year, which will be topped up to £3,600 by the government through tax relief. Your child won't be able to access the money until they're at least aged 55 (under current legislation) but because the money will be invested for such a long period of time, there is a lot of potential for any money contributed to grow substantially. And just like investment trusts, there's no income or capital gains tax to pay on them.

Children and tax

Children have to pay tax in just the same way as adults. In the 2015/16 tax year, they can earn up to £10,600 tax-free from any income, savings or investments. Because most children don't use up their allowance, the interest they generate from any savings is tax-free. If your child won't earn more than the allowance, you can make sure interest will be paid without tax being deducted automatically by filling out HM Revenue and Customs' R85 form, usually available from your bank or building society. Alternatively, if tax has already been deducted, you can claim it back by filling out an R40 form instead.

Protect yourself and your family

It's easy to live life in a little bubble, floating between work and home without a care in the world, rarely giving a second's thought to the potential pitfalls or disasters that may lie in wait. No one likes to imagine the worst but the awful reality is that burglaries do happen, people do get sick and we do sometimes crash our cars.

This is where protection comes in. The stereotype of the weaselly insurance salesman, skulking from door to door selling overpriced, unnecessary insurance, is fast becoming a myth these days. Many of us now buy our insurance online, using a price comparison website to find the cheapest cover.

While you can still purchase an insurance policy over the phone or, if you choose, at your bank or building society, the internet has revolutionised the customer-facing insurance business to such an extent that we'll look first at the pros and cons of online comparison websites. So if you are one of the millions who purchase cover via this avenue, you'll do so armed with all the knowledge you need to make the right decision.

Shopping for insurance online

Price comparison websites promise to save us time and money by producing the best quotes from a range of insurers – meaning that we no longer have to trawl individual companies to obtain the quotes ourselves. Bonus!

However, while they are certainly convenient and straightforward to use, consumers cannot always be sure that a comparison website will produce the most competitive car or home insurance quote. There are a few reasons for this.

First, not all insurance companies agree to list their products on comparison sites because they must pay to do so (usually passing on a small cut of the premiums to the website). Aviva and Direct Line are two such high-profile examples. This means that comparison sites are not able to search the whole market and cannot always be guaranteed to generate the most competitive quote.

Second, comparison websites will sometimes produce a quote that is not as competitive as the same company can provide you with if you deal with it directly.

Third, some comparison websites are able to produce better-priced quotes than other comparison websites.

Finally, comparison sites often highlight only the deals they make commission on – so you might have to check further to find more competitive quotes that the website has 'hidden'.

All of the above means that consumers should perform the same search across a number of comparison websites, plus obtain quotes from companies that do not appear on them, to be certain they are getting the best quote from the entire insurance market.

Of course, not many of us can be bothered to do that and we use comparison websites knowing that while we might not get the cheapest possible quote that exists, we're saving a lot of time and effort. Convenience is king in today's world, after all.

Learn how to use a comparison site

Comparison sites have many universal features and it pays to get to grips with these as soon as possible. One is the 'excess slider', the feature that allows you to choose how much excess you don't mind paying before any potential claim becomes eligible. The rule is the higher the excess, the cheaper the annual premium.

Comparison sites also usually have a number of pre-ticked boxes that rely on certain assumptions because they help speed up the search process. For example, when searching for a home insurance policy, boxes relating to the type of window or door locks you have are often pre-ticked. Make sure you check what has been ticked so you can be certain you are not giving wrong information about yourself that may later cause a claim to be rejected.

Similarly, as comparison websites are aimed at the mass market, they may not cater for requirements that fall outside the norm. If you have non-standard requirements (such as a medical condition, or a lodger), make sure you do not leave boxes ticked that claim otherwise and make sure the comparison website, and any subsequent policy you find, covers you fully.

Comparison websites have a tendency to force us into making decisions based purely on price. However, it might be more important for you to know the insurer is speedy at paying out claims, or covers you for a particular medical condition. So let price be a factor but always make sure you've got everything else covered.

It's worth noting that buying insurance online should increase savings, because many firms offer web discounts. Moreover, you should always opt to pay the whole year upfront, as many insurers charge extra for paying in monthly instalments.

Home insurance

Failing to have home insurance in place could leave you at risk if you're burgled and can also cover your possessions against accidental damage – those excruciating moments when you spill tomato soup all over your Chesterfield sofa or Fido leaves a nasty deposit on your cream Saxony carpet.

Buildings insurance covers your house for any accidental damage that requires building work to be carried out, such as damage from a fire, vandalism or flooding, whereas contents insurance allows you to protect your possessions and many movable objects in your home.

While contents insurance is available to both homeowners and renters, buildings insurance needs to be taken out only by homeowners.

There have been reports that during a recession, when household budgets are stretched, people cancel their home insurance but the effects of a burglary or structural damage to your home can be far more costly. In the worst-case scenario, you could even lose your home. So never leave yourself underinsured.

Let's look at the two main types of home insurance more closely.

Contents insurance

This type of cover does exactly what it says on the tin: it covers the contents of your home against theft and accidental damage. It may also insure certain possessions (laptops, smartphones, jewellery, cycles) outside the home, although you would usually expect to pay an additional premium for this.

Sometimes, including the likes of a smartphone on your home contents insurance is cheaper than taking out standalone mobile phone insurance – with the cost of the latest smartphones reaching £700-plus, this may be worth looking into at the time you take out your policy. (Equally, don't double up and cover this kind of possession twice.)

Things to watch out for include the following:

- Some insurers offer a new-for old policy that meets the replacement or repair cost of any items; others offer an indemnity policy that replaces exactly what was there before.

- Check you are happy with the excess and check the maximum payout on individual items.

- Check whether your kitchen fittings and appliances are covered.

- Be honest: making a mistake when you take out a policy could come back to haunt you. So don't say you have a burglar alarm when you don't or you could find your claim is rejected and you're left seriously out of pocket.

- Covering your possessions for accidental damage will increase your home insurance quote, as will extending your policy to include protection for items away from the home.

- When you apply for home insurance, the provider might check your credit record, and if you aren't on the electoral roll it may classify you as high-risk and bump up your premium. So get yourself on the electoral register just in case.

- You might not consider yourself a curtain-twitcher but by joining your local Neighbourhood Watch scheme you might reduce your premium slightly. Fitting a burglar alarm can also cut 5% off your home insurance quote, while fitting industry-standard locks is a good idea.

- If you use your property as a business, then you will need to compare home insurance policies that cover working from home – otherwise items such as stock might not be covered.

- Do you have a shed or garage? Consider whether you want your contents insurance to cover these outbuildings as well as minor possessions within them such as tools and lawnmowers.

- If you've got student-age children, it often makes sense to include their possessions away from home on your contents insurance policy, as this is usually cheaper than them taking out specific student insurance. You might not be able to prevent your Rory or Natalie from drinking in the student bar but at least you'll know their iPads are protected from theft.

Buildings insurance

This covers the structure and fabric of your property – the bricks and mortar, as it were, rather than the contents. If you have a mortgage, the lender will insist you have a suitable buildings insurance policy in place and many offer their own policies, although these are rarely as cheap as the policies you can get elsewhere.

The sum you insure, or the rebuild cost, is not the actual market value of your home but rather the amount it would cost to rebuild your home from scratch should it get blown away in a freak storm or subside after flooding.

So don't overestimate the rebuilding cost and accidentally supply your insurer with the market value of your home: you'll pay a fortune for cover if you do. You can find the rebuild cost of your home on your mortgage documents.

Flooding

The UK's home insurance policies are unique in Europe because they automatically include flood cover. Elsewhere, this cover is bought separately and is either partly or wholly underwritten by the government. It means that in the event of major flooding, an emergency relief fund is released that is paid for through taxes.

But up to 500,000 homeowners in the UK's flood-risk areas are in a more vulnerable position. In 2008, insurers agreed a 'statement of principles' with the government to renew the agreement it has to ensure flood victims can remain insured, albeit at a high premium with high excesses. This agreement was originally due to expire in 2013 but was extended into the summer of 2015.

Trade body the Association of British Insurers (ABI) has proposed a scheme (known as 'Flood Re') that involved adding a levy to every home policy in the UK to help pay for the cost of insuring flood-risk properties. The government intends to accept this proposal (at the time of writing), which means that homeowners in at-risk areas should continue to be covered.

Car insurance

In the past decade, motor insurance premiums have rocketed, driven mainly by the increasing number of claims being submitted by younger drivers, as well as claims for whiplash and the rise of 'crash for cash' scams. That said, premiums have been falling slowly again since late 2012.

Whatever the cost, you should never ditch your cover just because it's expensive – it's illegal to drive without insurance. Instead, look at how you can cut the cost. Here are some tips that will help you find the cheapest and, more importantly, the most suitable policy.

- If you already have car insurance, make sure you take a close look at the renewal quote your provider offers you. Do not automatically accept a quote from your existing provider without checking if you're getting the best deal. Insurers know most customers will renew their policies year after year, so they don't have to fight to keep your business. Don't fall for it!

- Also, don't assume you have to wait until renewal time to compare car insurance quotes, because if you haven't claimed on your policy most insurers will let you cancel with a pro rata refund.

- You can cut your insurance cost by keeping your car safe and secure: increase security by keeping your car off the road at night in a garage or on a drive, and by fitting an alarm or immobiliser.

- Lower mileage = lower premiums. So try to limit your mileage by car pooling, for example, or investing in a bike for shorter journeys. But don't be tempted to lie about your mileage, as this may invalidate your insurance should you need to make a claim.

- Once again, consider raising your excess, as this will lower your premiums. You should make sure you could still afford to pay out the higher excess in the case of an accident.

- It costs to be cool. If you're driving a Porsche or a gas-guzzling 4x4, you could easily save money on insurance by downgrading to a smaller, slower car. Vehicles with larger engines and body modifications, such as alloy wheels, are more expensive to insure compared with cars with smaller engines and less racy vehicles.

- Adding a cohabiting partner can also cut costs, and the same applies to young drivers who add a responsible parent with a clean, safe driving record. Make sure the person named as the main policyholder is the principal driver, as it is fraud to lie about this.

- Women used to be able to get cheaper car insurance but an EU ruling in 2010 means insurers can no longer offer preferential rates to women.

Once you've followed these tips and found a cheaper policy than the renewal quote offered by your existing insurer, ask if it will reduce its quote in a bid to keep your business. You may be surprised at how often providers can be haggled down to a price you're happy with, meaning you can avoid having to make the switch after all.

Travel insurance

The rise of low-cost airlines means that many of us no longer take a single, two-week holiday during the summer. Instead, we're at it all year long: Christmas shopping breaks in New York, ski trips, a quick week of sun on a Spanish island in spring.

Whether you take multiple trips during the year or enjoy just a single holiday overseas, travel insurance is crucial. It can cost thousands of pounds to treat illness or accidents abroad, while if you are seriously injured or ill you can face a bill in the tens of thousands. The cost can rise even further if, say, you need to be airlifted by helicopter from a mountain following a nasty ski accident. Can you afford to take the risk?

Travel insurance should be one of the first things you purchase following the booking of your holiday – and it needn't be expensive. There are two main types of travel insurance: single-trip policies, which only cover one trip; or annual multi-trip policies, which cover you for every trip you make over the course of a year.

Before we get into our top travel insurance tips, a word about your health because this is crucial. You must be upfront and honest about any pre-existing medical complaints, because non-disclosure could result in your claim being rejected. So if you fail to tell your insurer that you have diabetes and are then struck down by a diabetes-related condition while overseas, your insurer could legitimately refuse to pay out. It might refuse to pay out even if you come down with an unrelated illness or have an accident.

Also, some policies do not cover pregnant women beyond 28 weeks, while some policies have age exclusions. Read the small print if you fall into any of the above categories. Remember: a medical claim might be rejected if you have been drinking alcohol, so enjoy those sangrias but look after yourself.

Another important point is that holidaymakers can't always rely on the European Health Insurance Card (EHIC). The EHIC, which replaced the old E111 in 2006, entitles Britons to the same state-provided health care as locals across the EU, as well as in Switzerland, Iceland, Norway and Lichtenstein.

However, there have been instances in which Brits being treated in an EU country (such as in Spain during the summer of 2013) have been refused treatment unless they either paid for it upfront or agreed to reclaim the cost from their insurer – even though they had EHICs. As insurers have to pick up hundreds of their customers' bills, some have warned that travel insurance premiums may have to rise as result.

Even if your EHIC is enough to treat your illness or injury, it won't cover flight cancellation, lost or stolen baggage and other incidents of theft, so the general advice is to take out travel insurance wherever you are going.

Here are our top tips to ensure you pick the right type and the right policy:

- If you are considering an annual multi-trip travel insurance policy, then think about where you are planning to go throughout the year. Insurers tend to offer either European cover or more expensive worldwide cover. It might therefore be cheaper to buy one annual policy for Europe and pay for single-trip insurance for more global adventures.

- While you're allowed to take as many trips as you like during the life of an annual multi-trip policy, the duration of each individual trip is usually limited to a maximum of 31 days. So check how many days come under the heading of 'maximum trip duration' when you purchase annual cover.

- Ideally, look for a travel insurance policy that includes £2 million of cover for medical expenses, £1 million for personal liability, £3,000 for cancellation, £1,500 for baggage and £250 for cash. This offers comprehensive cover that should see you compensated in almost every eventuality.

- However, if you're a thrill-seeking, daredevil type, you'll need to bolt on additional cover to insure against mishaps on the ski slopes or during any other high-risk activity, such as scuba diving or paragliding. Adding winter and dangerous sports cover to your annual travel insurance policy could see your premium jump by 35%, so it might be worth taking out a specialist single-trip policy to cover a particular holiday.

- Check whether your policy has cancellation cover (and whether it is enough) as well as baggage cover, though remember it can be hard to claim for items lost or stolen when abroad.

- If you are travelling with your partner and children, then consider a family travel insurance policy. Check with your insurer to see if it will cover your children if they travel without you – on a school trip, for example. Also, check if you're covered if one parent needs to stay behind and one go home early, for example with a sick child; or if one (or both) parents wishes to head overseas without the kids at any point.

- Again, the level of excess you opt for will affect your premium; the more you are prepared to pay, the lower your premium will be.

- Some insurers now include airline failure cover as standard but make sure you check the small print. If they don't, then adding this cover to your travel insurance could cost just £7 for an annual policy. It could make sense if we fall into recession once again and travel companies go bust.

Life insurance

Most young people rarely think about life insurance – for good reason: they rarely have dependants or own a property. But, as we get older, we tend to accumulate houses, partners and children – and all of these need to be protected should the worst happen.

When we die, ideally we want to ensure our loved ones will be provided for and, just as importantly, that they won't be left with any debt. This makes life insurance a must for many of us. But there are, of course, factors you must think about when choosing a policy.

First, you need to understand these different types of cover before you can choose the best life insurance for you and your family:

- Simple level term insurance lasts for a set number of years and pays out if you die during that term

- Decreasing term insurance – sometimes known as a 'mortgage protection insurance' – decreases the amount of cover as you pay off more of your mortgage

- Family income policies are similar but pay an annual income for the remainder of the period covered

- Whole-of-life insurance covers you for the rest of your life, rather than a set term.

And, before you can compare life insurance policies, you'll need to choose between single-life cover (just you) or a joint policy that covers you and a partner. Joint policies are the most common because, when either one of you die, the policy pays out, making it simple and suited to most couples.

You can, if you wish, take out two separate policies. This will cost more than a joint policy but you will get two payouts instead of one. Couples with children often like to buy a policy each because it offers greater financial security.

Do the sums

Before buying a policy, work out how much cover you need before you obtain a life insurance quote. First, add up your outstanding mortgage and other debt; then work out how much your dependants might need to cover any other expenses such as school or university fees. Think about any cover you already have, such as death in service benefits you might have through your employer. Subtract the latter from the former and you should have a figure you need to cover your dependants in the event of the worst happening.

Also, the earlier you take out insurance, the cheaper your premiums – as long as you take out a guaranteed policy, which means your premium will remain the same throughout the term. When you're younger, you're usually healthier and fitter, and so are a lower-risk client – arguably the optimum time to find the best life insurance policy.

Remember to take inflation into account, as the real value of your payout will be reduced over time. You can take out an index-linked policy to ensure its value keeps up with inflation.

Finally, if you are concerned that your estate might be subject to inheritance tax when you die, then consider putting your life insurance into a trust. This will ensure the payout goes to the person, or people, you intend it to, rather than the government.

Health insurance

It would be nice to think that we all live a robust, healthy life before falling down dead at the age of 105. Sadly, that's not the future for most of us, and the majority will experience some form of serious illness at some point in their life.

Health insurance gives you the peace of mind that, if you need medical care, you can be seen by a specialist of your choice in privacy and comfort at a time that suits you. But there are a whole host of factors you need to understand before you can compare health insurance policies and choose the best health insurance cover for you.

Like any other insurance policy, you'll pay a monthly or annual premium for cover. In return, the insurer will cover the cost of private medical treatment should you become ill. The type of treatment covered by the plan will vary, depending on the type of health insurance quote you get.

First, learn about what is commonly covered. Healthcare plans are designed to pick up the tab for just about anything, from your initial consultation and diagnostic tests – commonly called 'outpatient treatment' – through to your treatment and hospital accommodation, known as 'inpatient treatment', when you're required to stay overnight. On top of this, and depending on the plan, it might also include physiotherapy, treatment abroad and cash payments if you have treatment on the NHS.

However, some things won't be covered. These include accident and emergency, cosmetic treatment, experimental treatment or drugs, long-term or chronic conditions, such as diabetes or asthma, and routine pregnancies. Pre-existing conditions are also commonly excluded, although some policies will offer a moratorium style of underwriting. In these plans, conditions will be covered provided that you don't require treatment for them in the first few years of the policy.

To compare health cover accurately, you need to understand the types of healthcare available:

- Budget insurance includes inpatient and day-patient costs but excludes outpatient benefits

- Comprehensive insurance offers full cover for inpatient and outpatient costs, as well as additional benefits such as physiotherapy.

- Intermediate cover, which fits between the two.

In short, the more comprehensive the policy, the more expensive the premiums.

There are also some slightly different plans where, say, 25% of your premium goes into a savings account that can then be used to fund some of your treatment, or plans where you receive a set amount for your procedure, scan or consultation and can pocket any savings you make.

The best way to obtain a cheaper health insurance quote is to go for less cover. A plan with little or no outpatient cover will be cheap and could be a great idea if you have the financial means to pay for any outpatient treatment you need. You can also plump for a larger excess to reduce premiums, while some plans are cheaper because they kick in only if the NHS waiting list is six weeks or longer.

Paying annually rather than monthly will cut between 5% and 10% off your bill and a more restricted hospital list can take 25% off, depending on where you live.

Cash healthcare plans pay out small sums for paid-for treatment such as eye checks and dental work. You simply send your receipt off to the insurer and it pays a set amount of cash back, depending on what level of cover you have. They can cost from as little as £7 a month for single cover to £50 a month for family cover. However, some critics claim you might be better off stashing your premium in a top-paying savings account and dipping into it whenever you need to pay a dentist or optician.

Critical illness cover

Critical illness cover pays a lump sum if you are diagnosed with a life-changing condition such as multiple sclerosis or cancer. While it's not considered to be as important as life insurance or income protection, it can be a useful add-on if you can afford it. However, choosing the cheapest policy can be a false economy as it may fail to pay out when you need it to.

If you've already got cover, you should review it to make sure it's still sufficient, and that you're not paying for something you no longer need. For example, if you've stopped smoking since taking out the policy, you could be entitled to a cheaper premium.

Be aware that definitions in newer policies are usually stricter than those in older policies. If you have a policy that's more than six years old, you may well be better off keeping that policy even if a cheaper one is available - insurers will charge more if you're deemed unhealthy and more likely to make a claim.

Keeping in shape and reducing your alcohol consumption can radically reduce your premium.

Making a will

Like life insurance, most of us really don't want to think about the inevitable but if you don't make a will, then you run the risk of your property, money and other assets going to the wrong people. If you have a family or other loved ones, then it's crucial you draw up a will as soon as possible.

If you fail to make a will, your money and possessions will be distributed according to the rules of intestacy. These are unbreakable state rules that dictate how your estate is distributed when you die - and will probably be different from how you wish your money to be divided up, as only married or civil partners and some other close relatives can inherit.

If you die without a will, and you have no dependants and are not married, your estate goes to your nearest living relative, even if you've not seen them for years.

If a couple is not married, even though they may have been partners for decades, then the surviving partner has no automatic inheritance rights when the first partner dies and could end up in serious financial trouble.

If you have children, you will need to make a will in order to specify what arrangements should be made for them if one or both parents die before the children reach 18. This may involve financial considerations but it will also mean spelling out who looks after them.

Despite law changes in 2007 that allow people to transfer half of a married couple's inheritance tax (IHT) allowance (£325,000 at the time of writing) to the other upon death (making the surviving spouse's IHT allowance £650,000), a will can still minimise the amount of tax you must pay the government – for example, with the use of trusts.

You can write a DIY will using forms downloaded from the internet but you should really do so in the presence of a solicitor who can talk through every aspect of your assets and how they can be distributed, plus any tax matters. You can do so for as little as £200.

In short, in order to be valid, a will:

- must be in writing
- must be signed and witnessed by two individuals aged over 18, who do not stand to gain from the will
- must be made by someone over 18
- must be made by someone with the mental capacity to make the will and understand its implications
- must not have been made as a result of pressure from someone else
- must start by stating that 'This will revokes all others'.

For more on inheritance tax, see page 151.

Divorce

Whether you've been married for months or years, the consequences of divorce can be financially devastating. Understanding how the process of separating a couple's finances works in practice can help save you time and money.

If divorcing spouses can put aside some of their emotions, divorce doesn't have to be an overly complicated process – assuming that there is goodwill on both sides and a desire to bring about a fair and speedy outcome. Every divorce is different but there are always four main financial points to consider:

- The immediate financial concerns of both partners – who will live where and how much will it cost?

- Maintenance – how much money might either partner need from the other in order to support themselves and any children, and for how long?

- The family home – who will get it? Or will it need to be sold?

- Savings and pensions – who gets what?

If both spouses are able to agree on these things amicably, it is entirely possible to arrange a divorce without the need for lots of legal advice. And in simple cases – for example, a young couple who have a similar level of personal wealth and haven't bought a home – it is entirely possible to divorce without instructing a solicitor at all. Instead, they might do better to collect the divorce forms directly from their local court and fill them in themselves. This way, they need only pay court costs (£410 at the time of writing).

However, if you feel that you do need a little help from a professional, there are ways to get some good legal advice for free, such as reading the specialist blogs of family lawyers or visiting the 'divorce surgeries' run by legal practices to help people who cannot afford a lawyer.

Alternatively, if your divorce is more complicated – perhaps you have children and complex financial affairs – and it becomes necessary to instruct a solicitor, you'll save yourself precious time and money by being organised and knowing what you want to get out of your divorce. For example, before you meet a lawyer, think about what assets you might want to keep and which you would be comfortable with your ex having, or selling.

The legal process of divorce varies across the UK but, no matter where you live, a court will try to decide what is fair to both parties and work out a settlement that best meets their reasonable needs. However, it will always prioritise the welfare of any children and their living arrangements.

When the court deliberates on a financial settlement, it will factor in the duration of the marriage, the ages of both spouses, their financial positions and their income prospects for the future.

It will also consider the standard of living enjoyed by the couple during their marriage, the contributions they made to family life (such as one parent sacrificing their career to be a stay-at-home parent) and then issues such as entitlement to benefits.

Who gets the family home?

Since this is usually the most valuable asset a couple will have, the family home is most often at the centre of divorce negotiations. When deciding what do with it, there tend to be three usual scenarios for former couples to choose between.

1. **Sell up and split the money.** While this may give both parties a clean break, it's not always appropriate. For example, if the property is mortgaged, then, on its sale, their share of any equity they had built up might not give both, or either, spouse enough money to be able to afford a deposit for another suitable home. Similarly, if either party is a stay-at-home parent or has retired or has no or little income, it is unlikely they would be able to get a new mortgage, so selling the property wouldn't be in their interest.

2. **One partner buys the other's stake in it** – or 'buys the other one out'. To do this, both parties need to agree how much of the equity they are both entitled to. If one spouse contributed more to the deposit or mortgage on the marital home, the divorcing couple

may agree that spouse is entitled to more of any equity that has built up. Once the respective amounts have been agreed on, one party may be able to raise the sum of money required to give to the other in order to assume sole ownership of the property. But if neither party is able to raise the money, scenarios one and three come into play.

3. **The spouse raising children stays in the house until the youngest child reaches the age of 18**, at which point both sides agree to pursue one of the options outlined above. If the property was bought with a joint mortgage and you choose this option, it is very important that you both come to an agreement as to who will make the mortgage repayments. Both parties will remain jointly and severally liable for the repayments, so if one party fails to pay the lender will pursue the other for the money. Some divorcing couples decide that the spouse remaining in the property will make the payments and the spouse who moves out of the family home will contribute money to the mortgage as part of a maintenance agreement.

Ongoing support

While your financial settlement might simply share the matrimonial assets between both parties in a clean-break arrangement, sometimes one spouse might need ongoing support, otherwise known as 'maintenance', for themselves and any children.

Spousal maintenance and child maintenance are, however, completely separate payments.

As for spousal maintenance, how much money might need to be paid to the dependent spouse, and for how long, will be decided by the court after careful consideration of both parties' incomes (present and future), their outgoings and the lifestyle they enjoyed during the marriage – which means the duration of the marriage will also be considered.

Maintenance can be set for a fixed period or on an open-ended basis, to be reviewed at a later date in response to factors such as retirement. Support stops if the dependent spouse remarries.

Child maintenance helps towards a child's everyday living costs. It's for children under the age of 16 (or 20 if they're in full-time education, but not higher than A-level or equivalent).

The easiest way to set child maintenance is for the family to make arrangements themselves for how much is paid and how often.

Sometimes, the paying parent may agree to give a regular set amount as a proportion of their income, or a lump sum to be paid at different points in the child's life.

If you and your ex can't come to an agreement, you can seek help from the government-run Child Maintenance Service (which has replaced the Child Support Agency).

In 2014, the government introduced fees to use the Child Maintenance Service to encourage parents to reach financial agreements themselves. These include a £20 application fee for applying to the statutory scheme.

The service has a free calculator tool that can be used to work out a family-based arrangement at **cmoptions.org/en/calculator**.

There is plenty of other information about divorce online but **gov. uk/divorce/overview** is a good place to start.

What happens to pensions and investments?

After a home, pension funds can account for a substantial part of a couple's wealth, particularly if they are nearing retirement age and have been making contributions for decades. But despite their financial significance, pensions are often a much less contentious issue during a divorce than the family home – an asset that evokes a lot more emotion.

Often, the couple agree to 'pension sharing', which involves transferring a proportion of the pension belonging to the spouse with the larger pension plan to a pension pot in the other partner's name.

Sometimes, the pension can stay in the existing scheme but is held under another name; in some cases, it has to be moved to another pension scheme and/or pension provider.

Bear in mind that you will probably have to pay administration charges to the pension provider to make the necessary changes.

The level of these charges can vary considerably depending on the type of pension scheme and the complexities of making the changes. The court order should say who will be responsible for paying any such charges.

If a couple has only small pension pots or investments and the income from them, or their value, is unlikely to be substantial, they could agree to trade them for other assets during the divorce, if appropriate.

In this tricky area of financial planning, it is advisable to seek professional advice from an independent financial adviser (IFA) before consulting a divorce lawyer. It will help keep the expensive legal costs down as well as give you chance to fully research your options and formulate the best possible financial plan.

How to find a lawyer

To find a reputable solicitor to help you get a divorce, if friends or family are unable to give you a personal recommendation, the Law Society's Find a Solicitor website (**solicitors.lawsociety.org.uk**) is a good place to start. Just select 'family and relationships' from the dropdown menu in the legal issue box, and enter your postcode. Look for members of the Law Society's Family Law, Family Law Advanced or Children Law accreditation schemes, which serve as quality marks, for extra peace of mind that the firm you pick upholds the highest standards.

Online divorce

While they're not suitable for everyone, divorce websites are popular among couples with straightforward cases who are looking to end their marriages quickly and cheaply. Indeed, one website says it can help you get divorced for as little as £24.99.

But before we go any further, it's important to note that what these websites are charging for is the admin – they will do all the paperwork for you. However you choose to get divorced, you can't escape court fees, which are currently £410 in England and Wales.

The service you receive depends on the price plan you go for, and there are usually three options to choose from:

1. A download of all the legal documents and some advice or a guide to filling them in. This is usually the cheapest option, at anything between £30 and £70. However, these forms are available free from your local court.

2. A managed service, where a 'caseworker' will fill in the forms and return them to court.

3. A managed service that comes with a 'clean-break order'. This is an order for a one-off payment, which relieves both parties of any future financial obligation to the other – as opposed to ongoing maintenance payments. This is the most expensive option and can cost between £150 and £300.

With solicitors' bills at up to £200 an hour, and legal aid largely no longer available for family law cases, thousands of people are logging on for DIY divorces.

However, while lawyers admit online divorce can work well for some people, they argue that the websites often put too much emphasis on clean-break orders in which financial affairs are dealt with at a single point in time and which make no provision for ongoing support.

They point out this fails to cater for people who may be ill, unemployed or are getting old.

Tips for a hassle-free divorce

- Keep channels of communications open. The process is much easier when both sides are able to talk to each other.

- Don't make rash decisions to get things done quickly. Think things through thoroughly.

- Be professional, not emotional. Be polite and calm when dealing with your ex and their solicitor.

Looking to the future

One of many people's great fears is that they will leave their children in financial difficulty or, worse, that their death will create a financial problem for their family. This is why, as uncomfortable as it may feel to broach the subject, you need to start thinking about inheritance and how you can ensure as much of it as possible is handed down to your loved ones.

Of course, tax planning is a highly complex subject, so by all means use what follows as a primer but seek tax advice from a qualified specialist before making any big financial decisions.

Inheritance tax

Inheritance tax (IHT) is a tax on the money or possessions you have accumulated in your lifetime and leave behind when you die, as well as on some gifts you made during your lifetime.

Rising house prices as well as a generation that is more financially savvy than the last – and thus will have invested more over their lifetime – mean that many more people's estates will be hit by an IHT charge when they die.

Once a tax for the wealthy, successive governments have failed to raise the IHT threshold to take into account the boom in house prices over the past few decades. Thus IHT, which is set at a flat rate of 40%, is payable on the value of your estate above the tax-free limit, also known as the 'nil-rate band' (£325,000 in 2015/16). So if someone dies with an estate worth £500,000, their beneficiaries will face an IHT bill of £70,000, which is 40% of £500,000 minus £325,000.

The IHT threshold in 2008/09 was £312,000, proving that the threshold for tax has hardly moved in the past six years. Moreover, the £325,000 threshold will remain until 2017 at the earliest, the government has confirmed.

At £325,000, many people's homes instantly face an IHT liability but if you also factor in the rest of your assets, including investments and your share of any jointly owned items, it's easy to see how IHT can become a big concern. Indeed, more than 4 million homes are worth more than £300,000, meaning that many more people are being caught out by IHT.

Crucially, IHT has to be paid by the beneficiaries of your estate before they can receive any of the money from it. However, just before the Budget of March 2015 reports of a possible rule change started to surface. Leaked Treasury documents showed that Chancellor George Osborne was looking to reduce the IHT burden for normal families by allowing property worth up to £1 million to pass on to the owners' children tax-free, which would effectively see the nil-rate band per parent rise by £175,000. So watch this space.

The transfer rule

As the current IHT allowance is transferable, married couples and civil partners are able to carry forward any unused nil-rate band from when the first person dies, to be used by the surviving spouse when they die.

It means that if Mr Smith died last October and all of his estate passed to his widow, when she dies, her beneficiaries will be able to use 200% of the nil-rate band at the time of her death to reduce the value of her estate for IHT purposes – £650,000 based on today's allowance. However, some people whose partner died before 21 March 1972 will be caught out by a date loophole.

Gifts

IHT is also payable on gifts you make during your lifetime, though the risk of this is reduced should you live seven years or more after making the gift. Whether they are liable for IHT depends on the type of gift you make. The following gifts are not liable:

- All gifts up to £250

- Most gifts to people made seven years before your death (see 'potentially exempt transfers' below)

- Gifts made by spouses or civil partners to each other – as long as both parties are domiciled in the UK. If either is abroad, the tax-free gift limit is £55,000

- Gifts up to £3,000 in total in any one tax year, known as the 'annual exemption'. You can carry any unused part forward but only to the next year

- Gifts to people getting married are exempt, as long as they are no more than: £5,000 from each parent of the couple; £2,500 from each grandparent; £2,500 from bridegroom to bride (and vice versa) or between civil partners; £1,000 from anyone else

- Charitable gifts are exempt, as are gifts to political parties, registered housing associations and community amateur sports clubs

- You are allowed to make gifts for maintenance (for example, if a husband, wife, civil partner or ex is dependent on you through old age or sickness)

- Gifts for education or training (for your children to attend full-time education).

Potentially exempt transfers

It is the person receiving the gift or 'potentially exempt transfer' (PET) who is liable to pay tax. However, the tax due on a gift reduces the longer you live after gifting. This is known as 'taper relief' and applies as follows:

- if the gift was made six to seven years before death, tax is reduced by 80%

- if the gift was made five to six years before death, tax is reduced by 60%

- if the gift was made four to five years before death, tax is reduced by 40%

- if the gift was made three to four years before death, tax is reduced by 20%

- if the gift was made less than three years before death, you get no reduction in tax.

If the seven-year running total of taxable gifts and PETs comes to less than the tax-free allowance (at the time of death), no tax will be due on the PET.

Strategies to reduce IHT

One strategy is to pass it on immediately. You can pass an inheritance on to your children or grandchildren immediately, if it makes financial sense, using a deed of variation. If you have inherited anything in the past two years, you can apply to have it redirected in this way. For example, if a parent died and you don't immediately need the money (and perhaps have a growing estate of your own that might incur IHT), you could use a deed of variation to pass the inheritance to your children or even grandchildren.

You can also use trusts in your IHT planning, as they allow you to pass money to your children but still keep a degree of control over it (in other words, prevent them from accessing it until a certain date). Seek the advice of a financial adviser and/or specialist solicitor if you wish to go down this route.

Reduce liability by investing. You can invest in certain assets that will help reduce your IHT liability. For example, shares in companies listed on AIM qualify for business property relief (which means they will fall outside your estate for IHT purposes but only if you hold them for two years). Investments of this type are inherently risky, so tread carefully.

Remember your pension. It is now possible to pass it on to the next generation free from tax. Previously, when pension funds were passed onto beneficiaries, a 55% tax penalty was payable, but Chancellor George Osborne abolished this on 29 September 2014. It means that no tax is payable when a defined contribution pot is left to a beneficiary, whether the deceased had withdrawn funds or not.

If beneficiaries spend the pension fund (rather than keep it invested as a pension) they will incur a charge at their marginal rate of income tax, but only if the deceased was 75 or older at the time of death. If the deceased was under 75, there's no income tax to pay.

You can give to charity (see page 161). People who leave at least 10% of the net value of their estate to charity, receive a reduction on the overall rate of inheritance tax payable on the rest of the estate from 40% to 36% – making charitable giving financially sensible as well as ethically sound.

A final option, of course, is to simply spend it before the government can get its hands on it but you'll need to spend it on items that are either intrinsically worthless or – as is the case with holidays, food and wine – worth absolutely nothing once they've been enjoyed.

IHT in brief

- Inheritance tax (IHT) is due when your estate and any gifts made in the seven years prior to your death, total more than £325,000. If an estate exceeds this amount, the excess will be taxed at 40%.

- Any assets left to a spouse or civil partner, provided that they are domiciled in the UK for tax purposes, are exempt from IHT. You can also transfer your unused IHT exemption to your spouse, so if you leave everything to them on your death, then there will be an IHT allowance of £650,000 available to their estate upon their death.

- Retirees are now able to pass on pensions tax-free if they die before age 75. For those who die after their 75th birthday, the pension will remain taxable at the survivor's marginal rate of income tax. The changes will only apply where no payments have been made to the beneficiary before 6 April 2015.

- Savers can pass on their Isas to their spouse when they die tax-free. The deceased's total Isa funds can be transferred to their surviving spouse's as an additional one-off allowance from 6 April after the death.

Funeral plans

Dying is far from cheap. Even when you reach the end of your life, some financial services companies will still see an opportunity to make a quick buck from you. According to Sun Life Direct, the cost of dying had reached an average of £8,427 by 2014 – 10.6% more than in 2013. The average funeral – including burial or cremation fees, funeral directors' fees and so on – stood at £3,590, a 3.9% increase on 2013 and an 87% increase on 2004, when Sun Life first began monitoring the costs.

The firm said that burial and cremation fees in particular were responsible for much of the cost increases experienced by the bereaved. Discretionary funeral costs (including the likes of funeral notices, catering and limos) stood at £1,833 in 2014. The most significant 'additional' cost was the memorial, at £772; though people also spent £150 on flowers and £373 on catering.

The research also revealed that almost one in seven people who organised a funeral in 2014 struggled to afford it. The average shortfall increased from £1,277 in 2013 to £2,371 in 2014. With these considerable costs in mind, it's well worth thinking about how you will pay for your own funeral, not to mention the funerals of your loved ones.

Dying is now the fourth-biggest expense we face after buying a house, getting married and having children. This is why many financial services providers offer funeral plans – but not all offer value for money.

Funeral benefit plans

These are often sold alongside life insurance plans aimed at the over-50s. However, they are expensive and you may pay more in premiums than the payout your beneficiaries receive. This is because, while the size of the payout is fixed at the point you buy the plan, your premiums could continue for decades until you die. A funeral plan might also tie you to a single, local funeral director who is not necessarily the cheapest in your area. A third factor to be wary of is that payouts are not index-linked, so they won't keep up with inflation – what looks like a sizeable payout today might not be so big in 30 years' time.

DIY funeral plan

Rather than opt for an expensive funeral plan, you could save cash monthly into a savings account yourself. It will generate interest and could easily grow to cover a funeral. You'll have to stipulate in your will that this cash is to be used to cover funeral costs, however. It will also allow your family to choose which funeral parlour and director they use and means they can better tailor your funeral to any specifications your will might demand.

Pre-paid funeral plans

Golden Charter and The Co-operative Funeralcare both offer pre-paid funeral plans. But there are a few tricky financial points to bear in mind. For example, while you can purchase a plan from Golden Charter for just £2,295, it doesn't include burial or crematorium fees.

Also, look into how the provider will let you pay: paying upfront should be far cheaper than spreading the cost over years. For example, Co-op's basic pre-pay burial plan at £3,265 costs the same if you spread the payments over 12 months (at £272.08 a month). But the two, three and five-year options incur an 'instalment charge' of 8% (£293.85), 13% (£489.75) and 20% (£816.25) respectively.

Writing a will

If you want to prevent problems for those dealing with your estate when you pass away, it's essential to plan for it now. Unfortunately, more than half of UK adults haven't made a will and 10% of them say that writing one has never even occurred to them. The figures, from **Unbiased.co.uk** and **Certainty.co.uk**, also show that more than two-thirds of adults in their 40s don't have a will, despite many of them having young families to support.

The high proportion of people not having a will is at odds with the rising number of people who expect to leave money and property to their loved ones. Indeed, 76% now plan to leave money to their families – up from 74% in 2012 – with an average value of £46,000. While 68% hope to leave property – up from 65% in 2012 – with an average expected value of £202,000.

However, without a valid will, those assets may not end up with the intended beneficiaries. Too few people are aware of the security a will offers and too many believe it should be written when they are older. Writing a will is about protecting loved ones, making sure they receive exactly what you intend for them and, ultimately, achieving control over your finances, even when you are no longer around.

If you don't make a will

Without a will, your estate will be divided according to rules laid down by the state, which might not be quite what you intended. These rules, known as the 'rules of intestacy', take into account your circumstances when sharing out your estate.

Intestacy: Married couples and civil partners will inherit under the rules of intestacy only if they are married or in a civil partnership at the time of death. This means that if you are divorced, or if your civil partnership has legally ended, you are not able to inherit under the rules of intestacy. However, partners who separated informally but are not legally separated or divorced are still able to inherit under the rules of intestacy.

If the deceased's estate is valued at more than £250,000, and there are surviving children, grandchildren or great-grandchildren, the deceased's partner will inherit the first £250,000, all of their personal property (known as 'effects') and half of the rest of the estate. The children then get the remaining half share on trust until they reach the age of 18. Under the previous rules, the spouse would only receive the income of the half share of the estate, which would pass on to the children upon their own death.

Example: Citizens Advice gives the example of Susan, who was in a civil partnership with Fang and they had adopted a daughter called Jia. Susan died without leaving a will. Her estate is worth £450,000. After Fang inherits her share of £250,000, the estate that is left is worth £200,000. Fang can have half of this, £100,000.

If there are no children, the partner will inherit everything – all the personal property and belongings of the person who has died, with interest on the estate from the date of death. Previously, they would have shared the deceased's estate with any surviving parents or siblings.

If couples jointly own a property, the surviving half will inherit the deceased's share, as long as they are beneficial joint tenants at the time of the death but tenants in common do not automatically receive the other person's share.

Example: In another Citizens Advice example, Tom and Heather are married and own their flat jointly as beneficial joint tenants. They have a child called Selma. Tom dies intestate leaving the jointly-owned flat worth £300,000, and £50,000 in shares in his own name. The flat goes automatically to Heather. This leaves an estate of £50,000, which also goes to Heather, as it is worth less than £250,000. Selma inherits nothing.

If Tom had owned the flat in his name alone, his estate would have been worth £350,000. It would be shared out according to the rules of intestacy, that is, Heather would get the first £250,000. This leaves an estate of £100,000. Heather would get £50,000 and Selma would get the remaining £50,000.

If there are children, but no surviving partner, the rules of intestacy dictate that the child or children inherit the lot (subject to possible IHT). All the children of the parent who has died intestate inherit equally from the estate. This also applies where a parent has children from different relationships.

Intestacy: who cannot inherit

Under intestacy rules, unmarried partners, co-habitees, lesbian or gay partners not in a civil relationship, relations by marriage, close friends and carers cannot inherit any part of your estate.

Intestacy: if there are no surviving relatives

Surprise, surprise: if there are no surviving relatives, then the government gets the lot. If you believe you have a claim on part or all of the estate or deserve a grant from the estate, you are able to apply. Look for the section on 'bona vacantia' at **gov.uk**.

A final word: when somebody dies without a will, families can go to war over who gets what, and usually the family fallout lasts forever. Few people would actually want that, so it's well worth getting a will sorted.

So rather than leave behind a potential intestacy mess, it's far easier to write a will and let people know how you'd like your estate divvied up.

Making a will

There are a number of ways to write a will, some cheap and some more expensive. At the cheapest end are the DIY will kits, costing around £10. These are fine if your situation is totally straightforward but they can still cause problems, especially if they aren't witnessed properly. For peace of mind, it's worth seeing a professional will writer or solicitor.

When writing a will, the requirements of the Wills Act 1837 must be met. These dictate that when a person signs their will, they must have two people witness their signature. You are not able to use the executor of your will or a beneficiary to witness it.

As well as giving you advice on how to draw up your will – for instance, carving up your estate by percentage rather than in monetary amounts – they'll be able to alert you to any potential problems.

These could include IHT planning issues, items that can't be given away, such as jointly owned property, and legacies that could result in legal challenges.

They may also suggest you write a 'letter of wishes' to accompany your will, especially if you're not sharing your estate equally. If this is the case, it's also prudent to talk to your family about your plans as this can prevent disputes and upset when you're not around to explain your decisions.

A letter of wishes isn't a legal document in the sense that it requires witness signatures but it will act as a guideline to the executors of your will on how you'd like things managed. This could include specific funeral arrangements and the gifting of sentimental items, as well as listing all your assets.

How much you pay to get your will written will depend on the complexity of your circumstances and who writes it for you but you can generally expect to pay anything from £50 to £1,000 or more.

It's also important to review your will regularly. At a minimum, you should check it every five years but also revise it if your circumstances change – for example, you get divorced, have a child or inherit a large amount of money. Also, your will is revoked if you marry, so you'll need to write a new one.

Will Aid

Will Aid is an annual fundraising campaign involving nine of the UK's leading charities. With the support of solicitors who donate their skills, consumers are able to have their will drawn up by a qualified professional solicitor while at the same time supporting charity.

Since being founded in 1988, Will Aid has enabled legal firms to raise more than £13 million for nine of the UK's favourite charities.

It works by participating solicitors drawing up a basic will for clients without charging their usual fee. Instead, they invite their clients to make a donation to Will Aid. The suggested donation is just £95 for a basic single will or £150 for basic mirror wills. Donations are then shared among the Will Aid charities to help people in need in the UK and around the world.

Before you search for a solicitor on the Will Aid website (**willaid.org. uk**), you should prepare for your meeting by using a will planner; you can download one from Will Aid and fill it in prior to your meeting. A will planner has fields for you to write in your personal details, plus details of your major assets (property, cars, cash, investments, insurance and pensions, for example) as well as any debt owed. You can also jot down your thoughts about who the beneficiaries should be. Then you take your will planner to your solicitor and they will help draw up your will formally.

Charitable giving

If you haven't considered leaving a gift in your will, then maybe you should. Gifts in wills are an incredibly important source of income for charities: and if your estate is liable to IHT, your donation will be 100% tax-free. So giving to charity is a chance to make sure your legacy lives on not just in the memories of your friends and family but also through the charitable work your inheritance will assist.

There are three types of gifts you can leave to a charity: a share of your estate (known as a 'residuary gift'); a fixed amount of money (a 'non-specific or pecuniary gift'); or a particular item (a 'specific gift'). A specific gift could include, say, a property or a piece of jewellery; a non-specific or pecuniary gift is either a set sum of money or a set percentage of the value of your estate. But a residuary gift – when you leave all, or a share, of your estate after your beneficiaries have received their share – is of most value to charities.

At work

We all work for one reason: to make money. OK, we know many of you love your jobs and do it for the satisfaction and warm glow that comes with a job well done. But, let's face it, we still need the money. Unfortunately, we don't get to keep 100% of the fruits of our labour. Instead, we have to give the government a cut to pay for public services – everything from building and maintaining our roads and schools to running the National Health Service.

So here's a run-through of the two deductions you've probably spotted on your payslip: income tax and National Insurance.

Income tax

How much you pay in income tax depends on how much money you earn. All UK residents have a personal allowance, which is the amount of money you can earn or receive each year without having to pay any tax on it.

In the 2015/16 tax year, the allowance is £10,600, (although those over the age of 65 may be entitled to a higher allowance) and this will rise to £10,800 from April 2016, as announced in the Chancellor's 2015 Budget. Your personal allowance can also fall, if you earn over £100,000.

So you start to pay income tax only once you earn more than the personal allowance – and the amount you will pay depends on how much you earn.

Those with a gross annual salary of £42,385 (made up of the £10,600 personal allowance and taxable income of £31,785) simply pay basic-rate income tax at 20% of anything over the personal allowance.

Things get a little more complicated for anyone on a higher salary. Those earning an annual salary of more than £42,385 and less than £150,000 are higher-rate taxpayers. They pay income tax at a rate of 40%.

Those earning more than £150,000 are additional-rate payers and pay tax at 45%.

Your personal allowance falls by 50p for every £1 you earn over £100,000. This means your personal allowance is reduced to zero if your net adjusted income (meaning after certain tax reliefs) is above £121,200 in the 2015/16 tax year. This is why the additional rate kicks in at £150,000 instead of £160,600 (as your personal allowance has been reduced to zero).

The tables below simplify who pays what.

If taxable income is NOT above £100,000…

TAXABLE INCOME BAND	TAX RATE
£0 – 10,600	0% (due to personal allowance)
£10,601 – £31,785	20% (basic rate)
£31,786 - £100,000	40% (higher rate)

If income is above £100,000…

TAXABLE INCOME BAND	TAX RATE
£0 to £31,785	20% (basic rate)
£31,786 to £100,000	40% (higher rate)
£100,000 to £121,200	60%* (higher rate plus tax trap)
£121,201 to £150,000	40% (higher rate)
£150,001 to £160,000	45% (additional rate)

(*where loss of the personal allowance at a rate of 50p for every £1 creates a tax trap)

Source: Towry, 15 April 2015.

What is the Pay As You Earn (PAYE) system?

It's a method of paying income tax and National Insurance contributions. Your employer deducts tax and National Insurance contributions from your wages or occupational pension before paying you them.

'Wages' includes sick pay, maternity or paternity pay and adoption pay. You pay tax over the whole year, each time you are paid, rather than paying tax in one lump sum. Your employer is responsible for sending the tax on to HM Revenue & Customs (HMRC).

Every time you are paid, you should receive a payslip, setting out exactly what you have been paid and what deductions have been made – such as tax, National Insurance and pension contributions.

At the end of the tax year, you will receive a P60 form that details the total amount you earned and what deductions were made in that tax year.

The PAYE system can also be used to collect income tax on any other taxable income you have, such as untaxed interest on savings or rent from a property you let out.

Your tax code

All employees are given a tax code by HMRC that employers use to deduct tax from their wages. The code is made up of a number, followed by a letter. The number shows the amount of income you have as an allowance that may be set against tax. The letter relates to the type of allowance(s) you are getting.

Common codes include the following:

BR	This stands for 'basic rate' – the rate at which tax will be deducted at if you have not been given any allowances. This code may be given when you start your first job and your employer is waiting for a tax code to be set up, or when you move jobs and your new employer is waiting for details provided by your P45.
DO	All your income from this job is taxed at the 40% higher rate (usually used if you've got more than one job).
L	This code is given to anyone born after 5 April 1948 who is eligible for the basic personal allowance of £10,600 in the 2015/16 tax year. It is also used for 'emergency' tax codes (see more on this below).
NT	You do not have to pay tax. This code does not include a number.

For a full list of letters contained in tax codes and what they all mean, visit **hmrc.gov.uk/incometax/codes-basics.htm**.

Emergency tax codes

If HMRC doesn't have all the information it needs to issue a full tax code – for example, because you've lost your P45 between moving jobs – your employer will be told to use an emergency tax code (ending BR) until the information is complete.

This can cause problems for low earners. Take the example of Michael, a student with a part-time job at a coffee shop. He works for only a few hours a week during term-time, and so earns less than the personal allowance, meaning he shouldn't have to pay any tax. Because it's his first job, HMRC was able to give his employer only an emergency tax code in time for him to be paid his first month's wages. So, in his first pay cheque, Michael finds only 80% of what he was expecting because tax has been deducted at the basic rate of 20%. While he will automatically get the money back in a subsequent pay cheque once the code has been updated – which may require a phone call to HMRC from either the employer or Michael himself – not receiving his full wages for his first couple of pay cheques could be very inconvenient.

You can find your tax code on your payslip and you will also be sent a 'notice of coding' to your home by your local tax office once a year. If you think you are on the wrong code, talk to your employer in the first instance. It should be able to contact HMRC on your behalf to get the code changed. If that fails, contact your local tax office directly. Your employer will be able to tell you which one that is. More detailed information on tax codes can be found at **hmrc.gov.uk** and **gov.uk**.

Self-assessment tax returns

Some people are required to complete a self-assessment tax return to tell the government about any income they receive other than their salary or pension. This additional income could come from rent you earn for letting a property or a room, money you make working for yourself, or income from your savings and investments. You will also need to fill out a tax return if you or your partner earn more than £50,000 and receive Child Benefit. Those earning a salary of more than £100,000 need to complete a return, too.

You must give HMRC all the details about the other sources of income you earn each tax year. It will then work out how much tax you owe. To do this, you must first register for self-assessment, which you can do online at **hmrc.gov.uk/sa/need-tax-return.htm**. Or you can call the self-assessment helpline on 0300 200 3310 for more specific information and advice.

If you want to submit a paper copy of your tax return, you must do so by 31 October, following the end of the tax year. For example, for the 2014/15 tax year (ending on 5 April 2015), the deadline for paper returns is midnight on 31 October 2015. HMRC will then calculate what you owe and set a deadline for payment.

Alternatively, you can file online by midnight on 31 January following the end of the tax year (so 31 January 2016 for the 2014/15 tax year), and your bill will be calculated for you automatically. Bear in mind that the online deadline applies to both submitting your return and paying what you owe.

If the amount you owe is less than £3,000, you may be able to repay the tax through the PAYE system via your tax code.

If you pay your bill late, you may incur a penalty charge. These are set at:

- one day late – £100* (even if you have no tax to pay)

- three months late – £10 for each following day up to a 90-day maximum of £900 (on top of the £100)

- six months late – £300 or 5% of the tax due, whichever is greater (as well as the penalties above)

- 12 months late – £300 or 5% of the tax due, whichever is the higher.

At the time or writing, HMRC was consulting on whether to take a more lenient approach to the automatic £100 penalty.

Further penalties apply in more serious cases of tax evasion.

You can also complete a tax return if you think you have underpaid or overpaid tax.

For help with self-assessment, consult your local tax office or Citizens Advice.

Change in circumstances

If your circumstances change during the tax year – for example, you have a new source of income – then you must inform HMRC in writing as soon as possible.

Digital tax accounts

Over the course of the next five years, HMRC will phase out annual tax returns as it introduces digital tax accounts for individuals and small businesses alike. HMRC says users will be able to register, file, pay and update their information, at any time of the year, using a digital device (such as smartphone, tablet or desktop) of their choice. The first accounts are due to launch in early 2016.

National Insurance

As well as paying tax, most workers also have to pay National Insurance. The money is automatically deducted from your pay cheque and, just like tax, goes straight to the government. The contributions you make, and which your employer also makes on your behalf, build up your entitlement to certain state benefits, such as the State Pension.

You pay National Insurance from the age of 16 when you are an employee earning more than £155 a week, or when you're self-employed and make a profit of more than £5,965 a year (with certain exceptions). You continue to do so until you reach State Pension age.

It's also possible to make voluntary contributions to make up for any gaps in your National Insurance record, such as if you took a career break to raise your family. This can be necessary as some state benefits require a minimum number of years' worth of contributions – including State Pension, which requires 30 years' worth of contributions (rising to 35 years from 2016).

Exactly how much you pay in National Insurance contributions depends on how much you earn, whatever your employment status. So how much will you pay?

If you're employed, you pay Class 1 National Insurance contributions at the following rates:

- 12% on weekly earnings between £155 and £815

- 2% on weekly earnings over £815.

Employees pay National Insurance alongside tax automatically through the PAYE system. Your employer deducts it from your wages before you get paid.

A director of a limited company may effectively be their own employee and so will also pay Class 1 contributions.

If you're self-employed, the way in which you pay tax and National Insurance is different. In the tax year 2014/15 (for which the deadline for paying the tax you owe is 31 January 2016), if you make a yearly profit of between £5,885 and £7,956, you pay Class 2 National Insurance contributions at a flat rate of £2.75 a week. However, if your profit is less than £5,885 a year, you might not need to pay if you qualify for the 'Small Earnings Exception' (for more on this, see the following table).

If your business makes an annual profit of between £7,956 and £41,865, you will have to pay Class 4 National Insurance contributions, which amount to 9% of your profits in addition to Class 2 National Insurance contributions at £2.75 a week.

If your profit exceeds £41,865 a year, then you'll also pay a further 2% on profits over that threshold (see table).

ANNUAL PROFIT	CLASS 2	CLASS 4
Up to £5,885	£0, but only if you get a Small Earnings Exception in advance	£0
£5,885 to £7,956	£2.75 a week	£0
£7,956 to £41,865	£2.75 a week	9% of profits
More than £41,865	£2.75 a week	9% of profits up to £41,856 and 2% over that amount
Source: **gov.uk/national-insurance/how-much-national-insurance-you-pay**		

Your work rights

Employment law can be very complicated and very dull. If we were to list all of your employment rights, it would make for a very, very long book, so instead we've pulled together a shortlist of the most important rights you need to be familiar with.

These are your statutory rights – the rights afforded to you as an employee by law – and nothing written into your employment contract can overrule them.

The most important six statutory rights you need to know are as follows:

1. The National Minimum Wage

This hourly rate depends on your age and whether you're an apprentice. The national minimum wage (NMW) in the UK is £6.50 an hour for adults (21 and over) and £5.13 for 18- to 20-year-olds, £3.79 for 16- to 17-year-olds and the apprentice rate is £2.73 an hour. From 1 October 2015, these rates will rise to £6.70, £5.30, £3.87 and £3.30 an hour. Your pay must be set out clearly in your contract of employment when you start your job.

2. Hours and holiday

These must also be set out clearly in your contract of employment.

First, hours. People who work full-time Monday to Friday typically work 35 to 40 hours a week. However, employers can legally ask adults to work up to 48 hours a week on average (normally averaged out over 17 weeks) – although there are some exceptions for which this can be increased. For example, people who work in domestic service at private homes can choose to work for longer, as can those who work in security and those who serve in the Armed Forces and emergency services.

Employers are not allowed to penalise workers who choose not to work more than 48 hours. For example, employers can't overlook them for promotion.

As for holiday, virtually all UK employees are legally entitled to 5.6 weeks of paid holiday each year. This is officially called 'statutory leave entitlement'.

The number of days is calculated by multiplying the number of days worked per week by the amount of holiday all workers are entitled to. Employees who work five days a week must receive a minimum of 28 days of paid leave each year (5 x 5.6 = 28), which can include bank holidays (of which there will be eight in 2015).

Part-time employees are also entitled to the same minimum of 5.6 weeks of paid holiday each year on a 'pro rata' basis – meaning in proportion to how much they work compared to a full-time employee. For example, someone who works three days a week is entitled to 3 x 5.6 = 16.8 days of paid leave; someone who works four days a week is entitled to 4 x 5.6 = 22.4 days.

However, paid statutory leave entitlement is limited to 28 days. So employees working more than five days a week are not legally entitled to more time off than someone working five days a week.

Unfortunately, self-employed workers are not entitled to paid time off.

Workers continue to accrue holiday while on other types of leave, such as statutory maternity, paternity and parental leave. For more on this, see page 111.

3. Parental leave

All parents who have been with their employer for more than a year are entitled to request up to four weeks a year of unpaid parental leave, up to a total of 18 weeks by their child's fifth birthday. This can be time for arranging childcare, picking new schools or simply spending time together as a family.

In the case of parents of disabled children, leave can be extended to the child's 18th birthday. And for the parents of adopted children, leave can be taken up until the child's 18th birthday or the five-year anniversary of adoption, whichever comes first.

Parents can take time off in blocks of one week depending on their usual working week. So, if a parent normally works five days a week, they can take leave in blocks of five-day weeks.

Workers should give their employers 21 days notice, in writing, before they would like parental leave to commence. Employers must have a good reason for turning down a request – for example that it would seriously disrupt the business.

Visit **gov.uk/parental-leave/overview** for further information.

4. Redundancy (notice and pay)

If your employer wishes to make your role redundant, it must give you a period of notice before your employment ends, the length of which depends on how long you've been employed.

If you have been in the job between one month and two years, the statutory redundancy notice is at least one week. This rises by one week's notice for every year you were employed if you have between two and 12 years' service. And if you have been employed for more than 12 years, your employer has to give you 12 weeks' notice.

If your employer wants to end your employment sooner, it can do so as long as it pays you for your statutory notice period and there is a 'payment in lieu of notice' clause in your contract.

If you have worked for your employer for at least two years and it wishes to make your role redundant, you are entitled to statutory redundancy pay. The amount you are entitled to is based on your age, how much you get paid a week and how long you've been in the job.

You will be entitled to: half a week's pay for each full year you worked for the company if you were under the age of 22; one week's pay for each full year during which you were 22 or older, but under 41; and one-and-half-week's pay for each full year during which you were 41 or older.

The weekly amount of pay you can claim is capped at £450. So if you are aged 35, have been with your employer for ten years and are paid £600 a week, you could be entitled to £4,500 (10 x £450) redundancy pay. Redundancy pay under £30,000 is not taxable.

There are some exceptions to the entitlement to statutory redundancy pay – if your employer offers to keep you on in a suitable alternative role that you refuse without good reason.

Redundancy is a complicated area of employment law and there are lots of strict rules employers must abide by. For further information, go to the government website **gov.uk/redundant-your-rights** or Citizens Advice redundancy advice guide at **adviceguide.org.uk**.

5. Pension entitlement

Under the auto-enrolment rules, all employees must be automatically enrolled into a workplace pension scheme by their employer if they are aged between 22 and State Pension age and earn more than £9,440 a year. Both you and your employer must make contributions to your retirement savings.

The minimum that must be paid in is 0.8% of salary for the employee and 1% for the employer but this will rise to a respective 4% and 3% by October 2018. The government also contributes to the pension through tax relief.

The auto-enrolment scheme, which was launched in October 2012, has been introduced in phases. So far, only very big and some medium-sized companies have had to enrol their employees automatically into the scheme but this will extend to all employers by 2017. This means you may not yet have been auto-enrolled and will need to request to join your company's scheme.

Employees have the right to opt out of auto-enrolment. For more information on pensions, see page 26.

6. Sick leave

Employees earning at least £109 (before tax) per week are entitled to Statutory Sick Pay (SSP) from their employers if they are too unwell to go to work for four or more days in a row. It's paid at £88.45 per week and can be paid for up to 28 weeks in the case of long-term sickness but it's not usually paid for the first three days of any sickness absence.

If you are absent from work for more than seven days, your employer can ask you to get a 'fit note' from your doctor to prove that you are or have been unwell.

Some employers have more generous sick pay schemes than the minimum they are obliged to provide as SSP, and some might give you your full pay for a set period of time.

If you have any questions about SSP but don't want to ask your employer, you can call HMRC's employee advice line on 0300 200 3500.

Benefits

There's a certain stigma about state benefits. Not all of them, of course – few of us begrudge older people receiving the State Pension, for example – but when it comes to benefits intended to help those of us who are unable to work (either temporarily or permanently), the social and political climate can feel somewhat different.

That can be unfair. Few people like to be in receipt of state help indefinitely. Unfortunately, for many of us – sometimes after years of paying tax and National Insurance – there comes a time when we need to rely on the state to help us out in our time of need.

If this happens to you, it's important to get all the help you can to ensure you are fully supported, receive the money you are entitled to, and can survive a difficult period, get back on your feet and manage to live a fulfilling life.

Many state benefits are available for people in work as well as those on a low income. Even the recently bereaved are entitled to some benefits, so the myths perpetuated by some elements of the media are unfair. They detract from the true recipients of the welfare state – people in society who need help from those more fortunate.

The benefits system is undergoing a huge shake-up after the coalition government introduced radical changes, particularly in the areas of Child Benefit and the State Pension, not to mention the introduction of elements such as the much criticised 'bedroom tax'.

The government has also introduced a 'benefits cap' that affects the total amount of support most people aged between 16 and 64 can get. It is £500 a week for couples and single parents whose children live with them and £350 for single adults. Plus the government is in the process of introducing Universal Credit, a new benefit that has already started to replace six existing benefits with a single monthly payment into recipients' accounts.

It has started to be rolled out but will not be fully implemented until 2016. Despite the changes, the key areas of state support include:

- Income Support
- Jobseeker's Allowance
- Housing Benefit
- Child Benefit
- Child Tax Credit
- Carer's Allowance
- Attendance Allowance
- Disability Living Allowance.

We will explore most of these here, but Child Benefit and Child Tax Credit are analysed in the Having a child section, from page 110.

Income Support

Income Support is intended to help people on a low income or with no income at all, who simply don't have enough money to live on. The amount you can get varies depending on your circumstances but someone with no income could get £57.90 a week.

Income Support is made up of:

- money for you
- money for your partner (if you have one)
- extra money for people if their expenses are higher than others (for example, if they are disabled)
- money for certain housing costs that are not covered by Housing Benefit.

You don't have to sign on as unemployed to get Income Support; it's also suitable for lone parents, carers, the sick, those on parental or paternity leave and pregnant women.

That said, to be eligible you must be between the age of 16 and the age at which you can get Pension Credit, and:

- have a low income
- work less than 16 hours a week (or have a partner working less than 24 hours a week)
- not be in full-time study (though there are some exceptions)
- not be getting Jobseeker's Allowance or Employment and Support Allowance
- not have savings above £16,000
- live in Great Britain.

The government will take your earnings into account when it works out this benefit, although there are some earnings it can ignore. For example, if you or your partner are working more hours than those above, you may still be able to get Income Support if, for example, the person who works is:

- caring for another person
- a childminder at home
- a part-time firefighter
- a member of a territorial or reserve force.

If you are separated, the state will take only your circumstances into account and count only the hours you work. However, if you think you won't qualify for Income Support because of the hours you or your partner work, you may be able to get Working Tax Credit. Plus you might be able to get extra Income Support for the interest on your mortgage or home loan.

Also, you do not need a permanent address to claim Income Support, meaning that even the homeless are eligible, as well as those in care homes or hostels.

How to claim

You can apply for Income Support by phone or by post. Either way, you can claim Income Support for yourself and your partner if they haven't already made a claim.

You can claim by phone – 0800 055 6688 or by textphone – 0800 023 4888. Those wishing to make a claim in the Welsh language can call 0800 012 1888. You can also claim by post, sending a completed claim form to your local Jobcentre Plus office.

Jobseeker's Allowance

Jobseeker's Allowance (JSA) offers a minimum of £57.90 a week to help those looking for work. There are two types: contribution-based JSA and income-based JSA. JSA is usually paid every two weeks into a bank account.

Contribution-based JSA

This offers £57.90 a week to those aged 18 to 24 and £73.10 a week to those aged 25 and over. But you can get it only if you have paid enough Class 1 National Insurance contributions in the past two tax years (see Chapter 10 for more on this). Also, your income or savings shouldn't affect how much you get, unless you are receiving money from a part-time job or an occupational or private pension.

However, you can get the contribution-based JSA for only 182 days (approximately six months), at which point you may become eligible for income-based JSA.

Income-based JSA

This offers a variety of weekly amounts depending on your current status:

Single (18 to 24)	£57.90
Single (25 or over)	£73.10
Couples (both aged 18 or over)	£114.85
Lone parent (18 or over)	£73.10
Lone parent (under 18)	£57.90

You can still receive income-based JSA even if you've not paid enough National Insurance and if you're on a low income but it is means-tested, meaning that your income and savings will affect how much you receive.

To keep receiving JSA, you will have to visit a Jobcentre office every two weeks – unless told otherwise – where you will have to prove you have been looking for a job. It's still referred to as 'signing on,' although the stigma of this phrase may have changed over the years.

If your circumstances have changed (for example, you have come into money or found a job), you must tell your Jobcentre immediately; otherwise, you could be committing benefit fraud. Bear in mind that you are usually allowed to volunteer and still claim JSA.

Am I eligible?

There are lots of clauses that may mean you are not eligible to claim JSA. You must:

- be 18 or over but below State Pension age (currently 65 but slowly rising to 67), although there are some exceptions if you're 16 or 17

- not be in full-time education

- be in England, Scotland or Wales

- be able and available for work

- be actively seeking work

- work on average less than 16 hours a week

- go to a JSA interview.

Also, to get income-based JSA, you (and your partner if you have one) must usually work less than 24 hours a week (on average) and have £16,000 or less in savings.

There are a few other rules, too.

- Self-employed: You can't usually get contribution-based JSA if you've been self-employed. You must have paid enough Class 1 National Insurance and self-employed people pay Class 2 or 4, too. If self-employed people do not qualify, they can get income-based JSA, tax credits or Employment and Support Allowance instead.

- 16- to 17-year-olds: JSA isn't usually paid to this age group or people in full-time education, except in certain circumstances. Contact your local Jobcentre Plus for advice.

- 18- to 19-year-olds: You can't usually get JSA if you are in full-time education or if your parents are still in receipt of Child Benefit for you. However, you may be able to get Income Support. If you have just finished education, wait until your Child Benefit ends before applying for JSA.

- Full-time students: You can't usually get JSA until your course has officially finished (check the date with your college or university). You may be able to claim JSA during the summer holiday if you have children. Also, you can usually do an Open University course or short course (two weeks or less) and still claim JSA – but tell your local Jobcentre Plus before you start.

- Part-time students: You can get JSA while studying part-time if you can combine your course with a job or are willing to give up your course for a job.

How to claim

You can claim JSA online. If you have claimed within the past 182 days, you should be able to make a rapid reclaim too, making it easier to receive payment once again.

Housing Benefit

Housing Benefit is intended to help recipients pay their rent if they are on a low income. You can apply whether you are unemployed or working and it can pay all or part of that rent although how much you receive depends on your income and circumstances. Housing Benefit can't be used to pay for heating, hot water, energy or food.

If you're affected by the benefit cap, your Housing Benefit will go down to make sure that the total amount of benefit you get isn't more than the cap level. That said, you may be able to get extra help from your local council in the form of a 'discretionary housing payment' if Housing Benefit doesn't cover your rent as a result of the benefits cap.

It sounds simple but Housing Benefit is quite complicated, so take a deep breath... There's no set amount of Housing Benefit. How much you get depends on: whether you rent privately or from a council; whether you have unoccupied rooms and live in council or social housing; and your household income and circumstances (including your partner's). For the purposes of Housing Benefit, your income is defined as money from savings (over £6,000), benefits and pensions.

You can't get Housing Benefit if your savings are more than £16,000, you live in the home of a close relative, you're a full-time student (unless you're disabled or have children), or you're an asylum-seeker or sponsored to be in the UK.

Council and social housing rent

How much you get depends on:

- your 'eligible' rent (in other words, what is considered a reasonable rent for a suitable property where you live)

- your household income

- your circumstances, including your age, your family (and their ages), whether anyone in the family is disabled and the number of rooms you don't use

- if you have to pay service charges – such as lift maintenance, communal laundry facilities.

The 'bedroom tax'

The so-called 'bedroom tax' (introduced in April 2013) means that if you live in council accommodation or other social housing and are assessed as having at least one extra bedroom in your house, your Housing Benefit could be reduced by 14% of the 'eligible rent' if you have one extra bedroom, or 25% of the 'eligible rent' if you have two or more extra bedrooms.

The reduction is worked out based on your eligible rent, not on your Housing Benefit. So if your eligible rent is £100 a week, and you get £50 in Housing Benefit and pay the rest yourself, then having one extra bedroom would reduce your Housing Benefit by 14% or £14 a week in other words – not by £7 a week, as that would be 14% of your contribution only).

So you can claim one bedroom for:

- each single adult or each couple
- each pair of children of the same gender under the age of 16
- each pair of children under the age of ten (regardless of gender)
- each disabled tenant
- each partner needing an external overnight carer
- all foster children (also applies when no foster children live with you as long as the room isn't empty for more than a year)
- each foster child that can't share a bedroom because of a disability or medical condition (though you'll need to contact your local council and supply medical evidence)
- each adult child in the Armed Forces or each reservist
- all external carers who provide overnight care for you or your partner.

Help with private rent

Under new rules, how much you get is usually based on the Local Housing Allowance limit in your area, plus your income and circumstances. The maximum eligible recipients receive is £250 a week for one bedroom or shared accommodation; £290 a week for two bedrooms; £340 a week for three bedrooms; or £400 a week for four bedrooms.

However, the new limits do not apply if you've been getting Housing Benefit since before 7 April 2008, unless you change address or have a break in your claim for Housing Benefit.

How to claim

If you're claiming for Employment and Support Allowance, Income Support or JSA, you can make your Housing Benefit claim at the same time via Jobcentre Plus. If not, you can get a Housing Benefit claim form from your local council or download a form from **gov.uk**.

Carer's Allowance

Carer's Allowance is worth £62.10 a week and helps you look after someone with substantial caring needs. You don't have to be related to, or live with, the person you care for but you do need to be aged 16 or over and spend at least 35 hours a week caring for them.

Recipients can choose to be paid either weekly (in advance), or every four or 13 weeks.

It's worth noting that Carer's Allowance is classified as taxable income, and it can therefore affect your other benefits (for example, if it pushes your level of income over the threshold below which you are due certain other benefits). The benefits it can affect include:

- Income Support
- Income-based JSA
- Pension Credit
- Universal Credit.

Because you can't normally get two income-replacement benefits (such as, say, Carer's Allowance and State Pension) paid together, an 'overlapping benefit rule' can come into play. If you can't be paid Carer's Allowance because of this rule, you have 'underlying entitlement' to Carer's Allowance instead. It's a tad confusing, but it might mean you could get:

- the carer premiums in JSA and Income Support
- the extra amount for carers in Pension Credit
- the carer element in Universal Credit.

Who gets it?

You might get Carer's Allowance if you:

- are aged 16 or over
- spend at least 35 hours a week caring for someone
- are in Great Britain when you claim (although there are some exceptions, such as members and family members of the Armed Forces)
- have been in Great Britain for at least two of the past three years
- are resident in the UK, Ireland, Isle of Man or the Channel Islands
- are not subject to immigration control (unless you're a sponsored immigrant).

However, the person you are caring for must get one of these benefits:

- Attendance Allowance
- Disability Living Allowance (at the middle or highest care rate)
- Constant Attendance Allowance (at or above the normal maximum rate with an Industrial Injuries Disablement Benefit)
- Constant Attendance Allowance at the basic (full-day) rate with a War Disablement Pension
- Armed Forces Independence Payment
- the Personal Independence Payment daily-living component
- If you're in any doubt, visit **gov.uk**, speak to a government benefits adviser or contact Citizen's Advice.

How Carer's Allowance can affect your State Pension

Usually, for each week you get Carer's Allowance or the underlying entitlement, you can also get National Insurance credits and contributions to the State Second Pension. (Previously known as the State Earnings-Related Pension Scheme, the State Second Pension is an additional top-up to your basic State Pension based on your National Insurance contributions – although you could also pay into it yourself. It is being abolished in 2016 to make way for the new flat-rate State Pension.)

The credits help to fill in gaps in your National Insurance record (which means you'll still be able to receive the full State Pension and other benefits) although they will stop being paid in the tax year you reach State Pension age, or if you get the underlying entitlement and Widow's Benefit or Bereavement Benefit.

Personal Independence Payment (PIP)

The Personal Independence Payment (PIP) was brought in to replace Disability Living Allowance (DLA) in 2013 for people aged 16 to 64 with a health condition or disability. You can receive it whether you're working or not and can receive between £21.80 and £139.75 a week (although it's paid every four weeks), depending on your circumstances – which will be regularly assessed. There are two separate components:

DAILY LIVING COMPONENT	WEEKLY RATE
Standard	£55.10
Enhanced (for individuals with terminal illnesses not expected to live more than six months)	£82.30
MOBILITY COMPONENT	WEEKLY RATE
Standard	£21.80
Enhanced	£57.45

For more information relevant to your personal circumstances, call the PIP helpline on 0345 850 3322.

Attendance Allowance

This benefit is very similar to PIP but is for people aged 65 or over. It pays £55.10 or £82.30 a week to help with personal care because you're physically or mentally disabled and you're aged 65 or over.

Which of the two rates you get will depend on the level of care that you need because of your disability.

Who's eligible

You can get Attendance Allowance if you're 65 or over and the following apply:

- you have a physical disability (including a sensory disability such as blindness), a mental disability (including learning difficulties), or both

- your disability is severe enough for you to need help caring for yourself or someone to supervise you, for your own or someone else's safety.

You must also:

- be in Great Britain when you claim (although there are some exceptions, such as members and family members of the Armed Forces)

- have been in Great Britain for at least two of the past three years

- be resident in the UK, Ireland, Isle of Man or the Channel Islands

- not subject to immigration control (unless you're a sponsored immigrant).

Medical assessments

The government insists on performing (controversial) medical assessments to check that you are eligible – or remain eligible – to receive certain benefits. You'll get a letter saying you need to attend an assessment to check your eligibility, along with details on why and where you must go.

At the assessment, you'll need to bring identification. You can use a passport, birth certificate, full driving licence, life assurance policy or bank statements.

Special rules if you're terminally ill

There are special rules for those who are terminally ill and not expected to live longer than six months, meaning you will be paid more quickly. Along with the usual application form, you must include a DS1500 form or send it soon after; you can get these only from your doctor, specialist or consultant.

How you're paid

All benefits, pensions and allowances are paid into your bank account. If your circumstances change, you will have to tell the government as it could affect how much you get. That said, usually your Attendance Allowance won't be affected if you go:

- into hospital or a care home for less than four weeks
- abroad for less than 13 weeks
- abroad for less than 26 weeks to get medical treatment for a condition that began before you left.

How to claim

You can apply for Attendance Allowance by post (use Form AA1A) or online. If successful, your benefit payment will be backdated to the date of your claim (usually the date on which your form is received or the date you call the enquiry line).

However, don't expect a speedy payment: it usually takes 40 working days to deal with your claim but it can be longer (or quicker if you're terminally ill).

PART 4:
Product Guide

Bank basics

We've come a long way from the time when humans first traded cattle as currency and established primitive banking systems. The ancient Egyptians stored mountains of gold in temples, while the Romans set up money-lending stalls in picturesque courtyards. Today, we track what we're spending on smartphones and tablets.

It was during the 17th and 18th centuries that banking as we understand it really took off, with money lending and the transferring of funds becoming commonplace. Fast-forward to the 2010s, and consumers have a huge variety of banking options, with everyday banking facilities available on every high street as well as telephone, online and mobile, with payments and transfers just a finger tap away.

Most consumers need somewhere to store, save and access their money. And the majority of us choose a bank or building society rather than stashing it under the floorboards. Here's the lowdown on all the ways you can access banking facilities.

High street banks

Banks are the corporate behemoths of the financial world. The overriding ambition for a bank is to maximise profits and pay dividends to shareholders, and as a result they are often criticised for acting against the interests of customers. High-profile issues – such as excessive boardroom pay and mis-selling scandals – have done little to dispel this sentiment. However, in a capitalist society, competition is king. This means that, in theory at least, banks should offer competitive rates to customers and the consumer always wins.

MONEY MADE EASY 2015-16

Sadly, this not always the case, which is why people should always check their chosen bank is offering decent rates and good customer service.

Banks tend to offer current and savings accounts, stock market-linked investments, mortgages, credit cards, loans and insurance products.

Building societies

Unlike banks, building societies are 'mutual' organisations. This means their customers are 'members' and, as such, have the right to vote and speak at general meetings.

The members own the society rather than shareholders. Because of this, building societies are free from the external stock market pressure that is applied by a bank's shareholders to maximise profits and deliver a return.

In theory, this means building societies should offer better rates than banks but in reality they are affected by the same global economic issues as banks and must ensure they do not fail as institutions, so they do not always compare favourably.

Building societies are also often regional concerns, offering a presence in areas that big banks could not justify servicing. This means local branch staff can offer a more personal service and local institutions often support the community through charitable initiatives – a bit like your local Post Office (if you've still got one in your village!).

Since the late 1980s, many building societies have merged or converted into banks. This consolidation, while ensuring the survival of building societies, wasn't necessarily good news for customers: less competition means less choice. For example, in 1900, there were 2,286 building societies in the UK; in 2013, there were just 45.

Funding is another big issue. While not so long ago there were numerous options available for building societies and banks to raise capital (such as borrowing from each other and from central banks), both are now somewhat reliant on savers' deposits to fund their lending activity. This is another reason why building societies cannot always offer better rates than banks.

Building societies do, however, offer a similar range of products as banks, with current accounts, savings accounts, stock market-linked investments, mortgages, credit cards, loans and insurance products all available.

Current accounts

A current account is simply a bank (or building society) account for everyday use. You can open one for yourself or you can open a joint account with another person – usually a partner or spouse.

Almost anyone can open an account, unless they have a history of credit problems (ie getting into debt, going bankrupt or a fraud conviction) but even then many high street providers offer 'basic bank accounts' that allow people to access a limited range of banking facilities.

Most current accounts are fee-free because the providers make enough money from overdraft charges as well as from separate products they cross-sell to current account customers (such as credit cards and loans – see from page 204). However, interest rates paid on credit balances can be low to non-existent.

Many of us forget to look at our day-to-day banking but choosing the best current account for your needs is an important decision. The following are the types of account you will typically be able to choose from.

- BASIC ACCOUNT: where you get a debit card (with limited use) but you may not have access to an overdraft or other credit facility

- STANDARD CURRENT ACCOUNT: gives customers a fully functioning debit card for use in ATMs (more commonly known in the UK as cashpoints) and shops, plus an authorised overdraft facility

- PACKAGED OR PREMIUM ACCOUNTS: where you pay for added benefits such as insurance and car breakdown cover, rewards or even interest on balances

- CHILDREN'S, STUDENT AND GRADUATE ACCOUNTS: offer added benefits for children, those in education or recent graduates

- CURRENCY ACCOUNTS: these are aimed at those who need all the typical banking facilities but might also need to regularly transfer money overseas.

Choosing an account

Ask yourself if you're the type of person who will remain in credit or regularly require an overdraft. If it's the latter (naughty), you'll need to find the best current account for low overdraft fees and charges but check how long you are allowed to be overdrawn for and whether there are any unauthorised overdraft charges.

Do you want to use a high street branch or would you be happy with just online access? Online banking allows you to manage your money from home and most providers have linked smartphone apps so that you can sort your finances on the go.

The best current accounts pay 5% (at the time of writing) on credit balances so if you do tend to have cash left over in your account every month, look for an account offering the best interest rate but bear in mind that some of these might be fee-based. Some accounts paying a decent rate might offer an introductory bonus, so check what the rate is once this expires.

If you're the kind of person who likes perks, compare accounts offering rewards: some banks will credit your account with, say, £5 a month if you remain in credit.

If you spend a lot of time overseas, bear that in mind when looking at the best current accounts for cheap overseas ATM withdrawals and purchases. Some charge more than others for using your plastic abroad.

Packaged accounts

Banks also offer paid-for accounts, where customers pay a fee for added extras such as travel insurance, breakdown cover and reward schemes. These typically cost from £10 to £25 a month.

However, packaged accounts have been heavily criticised because the added benefits are often not worth the cost. In early 2013, the City regulator, the Financial Conduct Authority (FCA), introduced new rules on these products to prevent mis-selling. Before selling customers costly packaged accounts, banks must now check that customers are able to claim on any insurance policy that comes with the account.

If you're interested, it pays to make sure you can at least take advantage of the benefits. With travel insurance, for example, you might find that the policy included in a packaged account covers only, say, Europe; clearly, if you're a fan of sunny holidays in the US or Goa, it won't be suitable. Similarly, cover bundled in with a packaged account might not include winter sports – not ideal if you're an avid snowboarder.

Also, before taking out a packaged account, check whether the same perk can be bought cheaper elsewhere. For example, if a packaged account offers mobile phone insurance, you may find it cheaper to simply add your phone to your existing home contents insurance policy. The same goes for legal help or commission-free travel money – two other typical packaged account offers.

Some packaged deals include identity theft insurance but your bank is legally obliged to refund you if money is fraudulently taken from your account anyway (and you haven't been grossly negligent).

If you are still tempted by a packaged account, ask yourself how long you might need the account, as many lock you in for at least 12 months.

For more on packaged accounts, see page 203.

Travelling overseas

If you plan on taking your debit card away with you on holiday and prefer to use it rather than purchase some local currency beforehand, bear in mind that you could be hit with a whole raft of charges. These include:

- Commission fees or a 'loading fee' of up to 3% of the sum spent, every single time your card is used

- A cash withdrawal fee when you use ATMs.

If you use a credit card overseas, you can be hit with additional charges. If you go abroad regularly and do want to use a debit card, check what your chosen current-account provider charges for the above.

If you use a debit card in a shop while abroad, you can also be hit with something called 'dynamic currency conversion'. This occurs when goods are priced in another currency but the retailer or restaurant owner offers you the chance to pay in sterling on your card. It is something of a legal scam, where the local retailer or restaurant owner makes a bit of extra profit – and can add as much as 5% to the cost. The retailer uses its own rate of exchange, which is far worse than the rate you would get from Visa, MasterCard or American Express. So always pay in local currency when paying by card.

Using an overdraft

Most of us stumble into the red at one stage or another but for those people who have not arranged an overdraft with their account provider, the results can be seriously bad for their financial health.

There are two types of overdraft: authorised and unauthorised (sometimes referred to as 'arranged' and 'unarranged').

With an authorised overdraft, your bank or building society approves your going overdrawn and agrees to lend you the money to cover this. An unauthorised overdraft arises when your bank has not approved your straying into overdraft territory.

Either way, when you go overdrawn, you are effectively borrowing money from your bank or building society – and you can expect to pay handsomely for the privilege. Typically, the fees for unauthorised borrowing are much higher, so anyone with a current account should be careful and always keep track of their balance.

You should think of getting an authorised overdraft if, by the end of each salaried month, you are frequently overdrawn or your account is near empty. But it is also important to remember that an overdraft is merely a safety net to stop you incurring even larger charges, and you should not be using it for long-term borrowing.

On arranged overdrafts, the charges you can be hit with include a monthly or even daily fee, as well as interest on the amount by which you have gone overdrawn.

This interest can typically reach 15 to 20% plus a monthly fee of £5 to £35, with some banks charging daily fees of around £1 to £2. If you continue to spend on your account, you could also be hit with transaction fees of £10 to £25 per withdrawal, direct debit transaction or card payment.

While some accounts charge a daily fee for going overdrawn instead of interest, this can work out expensive for smaller overdrafts, even if it is easier to understand. A one-day charge of £1 on a £500 overdraft, for example, is the equivalent interest rate of 73%.

Charges on unauthorised overdrafts can be exorbitant and can increase daily too, so avoid straying into the red without permission at all times.

If you have an overdraft, make sure you know what its limits are; ideally, you won't stray over this limit and will therefore not have to pay any added charges.

QUICK POINTERS FOR AVOIDING OVERDRAFT FEES:

- Stay within your limit
- Don't ignore seemingly small fees and charges – they can mount up (see the following table)

- Check payment timings – if any regular payments go out of your account just before you get paid, see if you can change them to just after payday

- Budget sensibly to haul yourself out of the red.

It's easy to overlook the impact of overdraft fees on your finances, especially if you've got an authorised overdraft facility and only dip into the red for a few days at a time. But if you're regularly borrowing money from your current account month in, month out, over the course of a year you could rack up significant costs. Here's how the fees charged by just a small selection of current accounts available stack up (pay particular attention to the Yorkshire/Clydesdale Bank fees!).

A COMPARISON OF THE ANNUAL COST OF AN AUTHORISED OVERDRAFT

	CHARGES	£400 FOR FOUR DAYS A MONTH	£600 FOR SEVEN DAYS A MONTH	£1,200 FOR 10 DAYS A MONTH	£2,000 FOR 12 DAYS A MONTH
First Direct	Interest at 15.9% EAR (first £250 interest free)	£5.23	£12.81	£49.66	£109.77
M&S Bank	Interest at 15.9% EAR (first £100 interest free)	£6.27	£18.30	£57.50	£119.18
Post Office	Interest at 14.9% EAR	£7.84	£20.57	£58.78	£117.57
Metro Bank	Interest at 15.0% EAR	£7.89	£20.71	£59.18	£118.36
Nationwide Building Society – FlexAccount	Interest at 18.9% EAR	£9.94	£26.10	£74.56	£149.13
Tesco Bank	Interest at 18.9% EAR	£9.94	£26.10	£74.56	£149.13
Yorkshire/ Clydesdale Bank – Current Account Direct	Interest at 9.90% EAR plus £6 per month	£77.20	£85.67	£111.05	£150.11

Source: **Moneycomms.co.uk**, *31 March 2015*

Keep track of your balance

The best way to manage your overdraft is to budget, keeping track of how much you're spending and how much you have in your account at all times. Online and mobile banking has made this easier as you can now track what is coming in and out of your account on a daily basis. If you are the type to lose track, create a daily, weekly or monthly budget that is accessible on the go.

Also, many banks offer a text alert service, which sends a text message warning you that you are close to passing your overdraft limit.

If you feel you are going to pass your overdraft limit, then speak to your bank. The banking industry has its own code of conduct that members should adhere to; under the Lending Code, banks have a duty to be sympathetic to your situation. If you communicate with your bank and let it know in advance if you're likely to go overdrawn, it may well be sympathetic and set up an authorised overdraft or extend an existing one at low cost.

Use your overdraft only for short-term borrowing or emergencies and try to avoid remaining overdrawn month to month. Overdrafts are not guaranteed and can be withdrawn at any time, so no one should rely on an overdraft or view it as a long-term borrowing solution – it's not your money, after all.

Managing your monthly income

We've all experienced that excited feeling as payday edges closer. In the last week before we get paid, the days seem to last forever and you've got less and less money to buy your expensive morning coffee from Starbucks until – wham! – you get paid again. Happy days!

Yet some of us learn to budget from an early age, spending only what we have and ensuring there is enough in our bank accounts to pay rent or mortgage, as well as living costs, and still have a little left over at the end of the month.

The best favour you could possibly do for yourself is to create a monthly budget, listing all your outgoings. But you have to be honest. There's no point pretending you only spend £50 a month on trips to the pub when you might spend that in one night. Same goes for haircuts, clothes and, yes, those morning coffees at Starbucks.

List all your incoming cash (for many people, this is their salary alone; for others, it could include benefits payments, child maintenance payments, etc.) and all your outgoings. This should include:

- Rent/mortgage

- Household bills (energy, water, TV licence, landline, broadband, mobile phone and pay TV)

- Debts (loans, credit cards, store cards, life insurance, car loans, etc.)

- Food

- Clothes

- Travel (bus, train, underground, road tax, parking, car insurance, petrol and MoT)

- Personal care (dentist, optician, prescriptions, gym fees, haircuts, beauty treatments, toiletries and make-up)

- Miscellaneous costs (vet bills, computer costs, cleaner, presents for others, treats for yourself such as books and DVDs).

Some of these outgoings will be monthly sums; others will be quarterly, weekly or even annual (if you include your average spend at Christmas, for example). You should divide these less regular outgoings to get a true monthly figure, then add it to your monthly budget planner.

If it looks as though your expenditure far exceeds your income, you will have to cut back. First, slash unnecessary spending, then try to eliminate expensive debt – if you are making savings deposits, it may well be worth you switching to paying off debt instead (more on this in our Debt section from page 73).

Also, make sure if you haven't already, that you have an overdraft-friendly bank account with an authorised overdraft. If you regularly go overdrawn, an account with a free buffer might be best as it means you will avoid paying for a small amount of authorised borrowing each month.

Fringe providers

Friendly societies

Like a building society, a friendly society is a mutual organisation. This means it doesn't have any shareholders but is instead owned by its members.

According to the Association of Friendly Societies (AFS), they were established to encourage self-help, sports participation and personal responsibility, and to enable people with limited financial resources to improve their economic status.

These days, most friendly societies tend to offer longer-term savings plans, investments or insurance, rather than day-to-day banking-type facilities, but a handful do offer the latter.

If you come across one, first check it is a legitimate business regulated by the Financial Conduct Authority (FCA). Second, compare the rates it is offering with more traditional high street banks and building societies. Only if it can better what you can obtain elsewhere and is a legitimate company should you pay it any attention at all.

Credit unions

A credit union is a local financial co-operative, owned by its members, which offers some of the financial services you get at a bank or building society. To join, you generally have to be living or working in the same area, work for the same employer or belong to the same church, trade union or similar association.

Many credit unions fill the gap left by traditional banks and building societies and will help out vulnerable people by offering them access to banking services. For this reason, they tend to be used by people with poor credit histories or no fixed address. You can get information about credit unions from the Association of British Credit Unions (ABCUL) website at **abcul.org** or the ACE Credit Union Services website at **acecus.org**.

What your bank will try to sell you

Sadly, the days of walking into your local bank branch and being greeted by a friendly member of staff who knows you by name appear to be long gone. Today, you're more likely to walk in and be greeted by a lengthy queue before eventually making it to a surly cashier. Greeting you by name? You've got more chance of the ATM churning out free £10 notes. If you're fed up with the all-too-common 'computer says no' attitude and want a more personal service, the grim reality is that you'll probably have to pay for it. What's more, your bank or building society won't just leave it at that; it will want to sell you a whole raft of other products, such as credit cards and loans, to tempt you into becoming a more profitable customer.

Here are a few of the things your bank might try to up-sell to you.

Premier banking

Premier current accounts aren't for everyone. They're aimed at high earners, or those with large sums of money in their savings or investments, and customers will have to meet minimum income or other savings and investment criteria to be able to open an account.

Because these customers tend to have more complicated financial affairs, premier banking accounts generally provide a more personalised service than you would get with a normal current account and come with lots of added extras. One particularly attractive extra is access to preferential or exclusive rates, such as cheaper mortgage deals.

Sign up to your bank's 'premier' service and you can generally expect to have access to your very own personal banking manager to help with your day-to-day needs. You may also get priority service in selected branches to save you the hassle of queuing, or 24-hour access to a relationship manager.

Some will run loyalty programmes, offering you discounts or invitations to special events. For example, one high street bank's premier current account customers can claim 'rewards', which give them access to hospitality at music concerts and sports games. Others offer access to airport lounges.

Such banking services can also come with the option to upgrade to a souped-up debit card. For example, some banks give premier customers access to a card that allows them to take out up to £750 a day from cash machines rather than the usual limit of £250 (subject to available funds).

You'll also usually get extras such as travel and mobile phone insurance, car breakdown cover and extended warranties.

The cost of premier accounts varies. Some banks offer their premier services for free to their wealthiest customers, while others charge monthly fees. For example, one bank's premier account costs £10 a month and has a minimum earnings threshold of £75,000 – or customers must already have £50,000 saved with the bank.

Packaged accounts

These current accounts are similar to premier banking services but they are open to almost all customers for a fee. The cost varies enormously from around £8 a month to more than £20.

While some accounts offer customers access to preferential exchange rates for travel money and overdrafts, the focus is on the extras, such as insurance, breakdown cover and identity theft assistance. For example, at the time of writing, NatWest's Select Silver account costs £10 a month and comes with all the usual suspects, including European travel insurance and mobile phone insurance, and a Tastecard that gives discounts at restaurants.

Packaged accounts have proved popular over the past few years and a fifth of UK bank customers has one according to the British Bankers' Association (BBA). However, packaged accounts have come under fire for not always offering value for money because it's sometimes possible to get the extras cheaper elsewhere and some 'benefits' aren't that much use.

It has even been claimed that some banks have mis-sold these products to customers in order to make a quick profit. The Financial Ombudsman Service (FOS) has received an increasing number of complaints from people unhappy with the accounts. Some customers said that they were ineligible for some of the insurance policies they were paying for; others have reported being switched from a free account to a paid-for account without their knowledge.

If you're thinking about opening a packaged account, or trying to work out if your account is giving you value for money, then ask yourself these questions:

- Do I really need the benefits?
- Am I eligible for the insurance?
- Can I get any of the benefits cheaper elsewhere?

Credit cards

Credit cards can be used to pay for virtually anything and there are more than 60 million in use across the UK, according to the UK Cards Association.

Most banks and building societies have their own credit cards and they usually partner with either the Visa or MasterCard payment systems. But it is the bank or building society that sets the interest rate, and any fees, charges or rewards. And when you pay your bill, the money goes to the bank or building society, not Visa or MasterCard.

Using a credit card is a bit like taking out a loan. However, unlike a loan, where you get given the full sum upfront and agree to repay it over a certain period of time at a set interest rate, with a credit card you can spend up to an agreed amount over a virtually open-ended period as long as you make the minimum repayments each month.

A credit card charges you interest for the convenience of being able to spread payments over time. The minimum repayment each month is typically set at 5% of the amount you've spent on the card, or £5 – whichever is greater. In 2012/13, the average interest rate –

referred to as the 'annual percentage rate' (or APR) – on a credit card was 17.56%, meaning that for every £100 spent on a credit card, the lender made a £17.56 profit over a year (unless it was paid off in full), and that's before any charges for late payment were levied.

0% purchase cards

Lots of credit cards now offer interest-free periods on purchases to compete for your custom and, as a result, the length of the 0% period is getting longer and longer. At the time of writing, the longest available was 23 months.

Interest-free purchase credit cards are a great way to spread payment for big-ticket items such as holidays or a new sofa because, as long as you stick to the minimum repayment each month and clear your debt by the end of the interest-free period, you won't spend a penny more than if you had bought the items outright to start with.

So what's in it for the bank? Well, not everyone repays what they owe on time and, at the end of the interest-free period, some customers who are unable to clear their balance end up having to pay interest. At this point the APR will typically jump to anything between 16% and 18%, and so the bank starts to make money.

To avoid this, however, cardholders could consider switching credit cards to a 0% balance transfer card.

Balance transfer cards

A balance transfer lets you move an outstanding balance from one or more existing cards on to a new card charging less interest. Often, the deal will include an interest-free period on the balance, which can be as long as two years (or up to 36 months at the time of writing). Some cards will also come with an introductory interest-free period on new purchases too but these don't tend to last long – typically for three to six months.

It's important to bear in mind that most balance-transfer deals come with a handling fee – usually around 3% of the balance being transferred – for the convenience of moving your debt to a lower interest rate. So moving a £5,000 balance on to a balance transfer card charging a 3% handling fee will cost £150.

However, if you're paying a high amount of interest on your credit card spending, you could still be better off moving all your balances to a 0% balance-transfer card even after the fee is taken into account.

Take this example from credit card payment company MBNA: Mrs Smith has a balance of £1,000 outstanding on a store card that charges interest at 26%. She is making fixed monthly payments of £20. The next day she takes out a card offering 0% on balance transfers for 12 months, with a 3% handling fee. She transfers the balance from her store card to this, pays the £30 handling fee and continues to make monthly payments of £20. Twelve months later, she will have made a total saving of £216.22. Even taking into account the handling fee, she is substantially better off.

If you move multiple balances on to a balance-transfer card, another benefit is that you will have to deal with only one lender and arrange just one repayment each month.

But don't forget: whatever type of credit card you have, if you fall behind with your payments, then you're likely to incur charges and your credit record (a file of your credit history used by financial providers to assess your suitability for a loan) may be adversely affected.

If you're worried you might forget to make a payment, you could set up a direct debit for the minimum repayment to be taken from your bank account every month.

Something else to bear in mind is that the APR advertised might not always be the rate you're offered when you apply for a credit card because lenders take your credit history into account. If you have a poor credit score, you might be offered a higher rate of interest.

Useful websites for comparing credit cards include:

- **comparethemarket.com**
- **confused.com**
- **gocompare.com**

- **moneysupermarket.com**
- **moneywise.co.uk/compare**
- **uswitch.com**.

Personal loans

Unsecured loans

Your bank or building society will often offer you the facility to borrow money through an unsecured personal loan. Typically, it will lend you up to £25,000 over a period of between one and seven years at an interest rate fixed for the duration of the loan. For example, at the time of writing, one lender gave customers the ability to borrow between £7,500 and £15,000 over three years at a representative APR of 4.8%. So if you were to borrow £10,000 over three years, you would pay £298.81 each month and the total cost of the loan over the term would be £10,757.23, meaning that the lender earns £757.23 in interest.

Some borrowers prefer unsecured personal loans over a credit card because not only are they typically able to borrow more money but they also know exactly how much money they will be borrowing over a specific length of time (the 'term'), what it will cost them each month and in total. However, one downside is that if you want to repay what you owe before the end of the agreed term, some lenders will charge you a penalty fee. So always read the small print carefully to find out how much you may have to pay.

While your home is not normally at risk if you can't repay an unsecured loan, your credit record could be affected, plus you might face a hefty legal bill.

Secured loans

If you want to borrow more than around £25,000, then your bank may offer you an alternative personal loan called a secured loan. Because you want to borrow a significant sum, to cover the extra risk of you being unable to repay it, the bank will take security against an asset you own – usually your home. This extra security means that the interest rates on secured loans are often lower than they are on unsecured loans. But be warned: default on your loan and you could lose your home. This is why you should never take out a secured loan unless you are 100% confident that you can afford the monthly repayments.

What is PPI?

You may have heard about the payment protection insurance (or PPI) scandal in the news over the past few years. This is because approximately 16 million policies were mis-sold to customers.

Payment protection insurance (PPI) covers loan or other debt repayments if you are unable to pay for certain reasons, such as being made redundant or taken ill.

Policies were often sold alongside loans, mortgages, credit cards, store cards and car finance. The trouble was that lots of the people who were sold a policy found that they were unable to use it. The financial regulator was – and still is – flooded with complaints and, since April 2012, companies have not generally been allowed to sell PPI at the same time as customers take out credit.

Compensation claims have already cost the banks more than £20 billion and complaints continue to pour in.

If you think you might have been mis-sold such a policy and want to find out if you are entitled to compensation, write to your bank outlining the details of your claim – including dates – in the first instance. If it agrees with you, it may award you compensation right away.

If your complaint isn't upheld, contact the Financial Ombudsman Service (FOS), which can assess your claim and, if it finds in your favour, make the bank pay up. You can call the FOS on 0300 123 6222 or 0800 121 6222 and find more information about PPI and how to make a claim online at **financial-ombudsman.org.uk**.

However, take note: if you think you've got a claim, don't be tempted to use a claims management company. It will take a significant chunk – up to 30% – of any compensation awarded in return for contacting your bank on your behalf, something you can do easily yourself.

Moreover, there are a lot of scam claims companies doing the rounds, so you could easily end up giving your financial details to a rogue firm. So steer clear of claims management firms completely and submit the claim yourself.

If you're unsure about how to write to the bank, you can find template letters at a range of consumer-friendly websites including Citizens Advice at **adviceguide.org.uk**.

PART 5:
Jargon Buster

Jargon buster

Active fund: an active fund has a manager at the helm (and usually a team of analysts and researchers) who will select the assets that they believe will increase in value. Actively managed funds have the capacity to outperform other funds and the market as a whole. They are usually slightly more expensive than passive funds because investors must pay for the manager's expertise.

AER: while the annual percentage rate (APR) is the rate charged for money borrowed, the annual equivalent rate (AER) is how interest is calculated on money saved. The AER takes into account the frequency with which the product pays interest and how that interest compounds. So if two savings products pay the same rate of interest but one pays interest more frequently, that account compounds the interest more frequently and will have a higher AER.

Agreement in principle: a conditional offer made by a mortgage lender to verify that it will 'in principle' give you the mortgage loan you have discussed with it. This helps speed up the house-buying process as it demonstrates to sellers that you're a serious buyer. However, it's not a guarantee the lender will lend you the money, as this will still depend on a survey of the property and the outcome of credit checks. The offer in principle will be valid for a limited time, typically up to three months.

Annuity: in exchange for any lump sum – usually your pension fund – an annuity is 'bought' from an insurance company and provides an income for life. When you die, the income stops. Annuity rates fluctuate daily and depend on your age, health and a number of other factors, so you have to pick the right one and, once bought, its terms cannot be altered, so seek financial advice.

APR: the annual percentage rate (APR) is used to compare interest rates for borrowing. It is the total (or 'gross') interest you'll pay over the life of a loan, including charges and fees. For credit cards where interest is charged at more frequent intervals, the APR includes a 'compounding' effect (paying interest on interest). So for a credit card charging 2% interest a month (equating to 24% a year), the APR would actually be 26.82%.

Arrears: tend to be associated with debt. If you fall behind and miss payments on any outstanding debt, the amount you failed to pay is an arrear – the amount accrued from the date on which the first missed payment was due.

Balance transfer: moving money from one account to another, whether switching bank accounts or more likely transferring the outstanding balance on your credit card to another card that charges a lower – or 0% – rate of interest. Some card providers may charge a transfer fee, which can be a percentage of the balance transferred.

Bankruptcy: a person (or business) unable to pay the debts it owes creditors can either volunteer or be forced into bankruptcy – a legal proceeding whereby an insolvent person can be relieved of their financial obligations – but loses control over their bank accounts. Bankruptcy is not a soft option. Although it may wipe the financial slate clean, it is extremely harmful to a person's credit rating (it will stay on your credit record for six years) and will adversely affect your future dealings with financial institutions.

Base rate: also referred to as 'Bank Rate' or the 'minimum lending rate', the Bank of England base rate is the lowest rate the Bank uses to discount bills of exchange. This affects consumers because it is used by mainstream lenders and banks as the basis for calculating interest rates on mortgages, loans and savings.

Basic account: a no-frills, or 'vanilla', bank account that allows you to have your salary paid in, to set up direct debits and standing orders for money going out and online access but won't allow you an overdraft, cheque-book, interest earned on the balance or paper statements.

Bonds: debt issued by governments or companies to raise money. Bonds promise a set amount of interest until the bond matures at a fixed date in the future.

Buildings insurance: this type of insurance covers the structure and fabric of your property – the bricks and mortar, not the contents (for which you need contents or 'home' insurance). If you have a mortgage, the lender will insist you have a suitable buildings insurance policy in place. Many lenders offer their own building insurance policies but you don't have to buy it from them; you have the option of shopping around. The insurance covers you for the rebuilding costs, not the market value of the property.

Building society: a mutual organisation owned by its members and not by shareholders. These societies offer a range of financial services but have historically concentrated on taking deposits from savers and lending the money to borrowers as mortgages, hence the name. In the mid-1990s, many societies 'demutualised' and became banks.

Buy to let: the catch-all term applied to investors who buy properties with the sole intention of letting them to tenants rather than living in them themselves, with the proceeds from the let usually used for the repayment of the mortgage. Buy-to-let investors have to take out specialised mortgages that carry higher interest rates and require a much bigger deposit than a standard mortgage. Other expenditure can include legal fees, income tax (on the rental profits you make), capital gains tax (if you sell the property) and 'void' periods when the property is unlet.

Child Tax Credit: a scheme started in 2003 that sought to replace a raft of other tax credits and benefits, the payout depends on the number of dependent children in a family, and its level of income. The amount of credit is reduced as income increases. It is payable to the main carer of a child, usually the mother, and is available whether or not the recipient is working.

Childcare vouchers: a special government scheme operated through employers that allows you to pay for childcare from your pre-tax salary. The vouchers cover childcare up to 1 September after your child's 15th birthday (16th if they are disabled) and can be used at any registered and regulated nursery or playgroup and for nannies, childminders or au pairs.

Closed-ended funds: a company that invests in other companies or assets. With a closed-ended fund, such as an investment trust, there is a set number of shares and this number does not change regardless of the number of investors.

Contents insurance: covers the contents of your home for theft and damage and also may insure certain possessions (jewellery, cycles) outside of the home. Things to watch for include the excess and also the maximum payout on individual items. Another grey area is kitchen fittings, as some contents policies say these are not contents but part of the fabric of the property and therefore covered by buildings insurance, while some buildings policies don't cover them because they regard them as contents.

CPI: the Consumer Prices Index is the official measure of inflation adopted by the government to set its targets. When commentators refer to changes in inflation, they're usually talking about CPI.

Critical illness insurance: this pays out a tax-free lump sum if you become seriously ill. All policies should cover seven core conditions: cancer, coronary artery bypass, heart attack, kidney failure, major organ transplant, multiple sclerosis and stroke. You must normally survive at least one month after becoming critically ill before the policy will pay out. Payouts are determined by premiums and premiums are determined by the severity of your illness – the less severe, the lower the premiums.

Current account: an account opened with a bank or building society that provides the ability to draw cash (usually via a debit card) or cheques from the account. Some pay fairly minimal rates of interest if the account is in credit. Most current accounts insist your monthly income (salary or pension) is paid directly in each month and they offer a number of optional services – such as overdrafts and charge cards – which are negotiable but will incur fees.

Defined benefit pension: often referred to as a 'final salary' pension, benefits paid in retirement are known in advance and are 'defined' when the employee joins the scheme. Benefits are based on the employee's salary history and length of service rather than on investment returns.

Defined contribution pension: often referred to as a 'money purchase' pension, the level of benefit is solely dependent on the accumulated value of the individual's pension contributions and their performance as investments. Therefore, the scheme member is shouldering the risk of their pension, as the scheme will pay a pension based only on the contributions and investment performance.

Dividend: a payment made to shareholders from part of a company's profits.

Early repayment charges: you may think a lender would be grateful to you for paying off your debts early. Alas, no. Mortgages and loans levy early repayment (or redemption) charges because the profitability of your loan or mortgage to the lender is calculated on the basis of the interest that you'll pay over the full term of the loan.

Equities: ownership of a company in the form of a stock (also referred to as shares), traded on stock exchanges.

Estate: everything you own, meaning all your assets (property, cars, investments, savings, insurance payouts, artwork, furniture, etc.) minus any liabilities (debts, current bills, payments still owed on assets such as cars and houses, credit card balances and other outstanding loans). When you're alive, this is called your wealth; when you're dead, it becomes your estate.

Excess: this is more usually a feature of car insurance but it can also crop up in contents, mobile phone and pet insurance policies. It is the amount of money you have to pay before the insurance company starts paying out. The excess makes up the first part of a claim, so if your excess is £100 and your claim is for £500, you would pay the first £100 and the insurer the remaining £400. Many online insurers let you set your own excess but the lower the excess, the more expensive the premium will be.

Exchange rates: the difference between two currencies – specifically how much one currency is worth relative to another. For example, if £1 is worth $1.50, converting sterling to US dollars, the exchange rate is 1:1.5.

Exchange-traded funds (ETFs): an equity-based product that can be traded as a single company but which invests in a range of assets like a collective fund.

Financial Conduct Authority (FCA): the FCA is the financial services regulator. An independent non-governmental body, it has a wide range of rule-making, investigatory and enforcement powers, which include consumer protection. It took over from the Financial Services Authority (FSA) in April 2013.

Financial Ombudsman Service (FOS): if you have a complaint about a financial service product you have bought but the company you bought it from refuses to resolve your problem after eight weeks, the FOS can help. The Ombudsman will investigate and resolve the matter; it is independent and its service is free to consumers. The Ombudsman may find in the company's favour but consumers don't have to accept its decision and are always free to go to court instead. But if they do accept an Ombudsman's decision, it is binding both on them and on the business.

Financial Services Compensation Scheme (FSCS): this is the compensation fund of last resort for customers of authorised financial services firms. If a firm becomes insolvent or ceases trading, the FSCS may be able to pay compensation to its customers – up to £85,000 for savings deposits in high street banks and building societies, for example. However, to qualify for compensation, the firm you were dealing with must be authorised by the FCA.

Freehold: permanent and absolute ownership and tenure of a property (residential or commercial) and/or land with freedom to dispose of it at will but with no time limit as to how long the property/land can be held (in perpetuity). Freehold is the opposite of leasehold.

Income protection insurance: if you can't work in the event of sickness or illness, income protection insurance aims to give you an income, with the amount of income set by you up to 75% of your gross (before tax) income and the premiums varying by how much of your salary you want to cover, as well as your age and health and when you want to start receiving any payouts. Any payouts from income protection insurance are tax-free and usually continue until you recover, reach your selected pension age or the period of cover specified in the policy comes to an end. Income protection insurance does not cover redundancy but you can buy such cover as a bolt-on.

Inflation: an increase in the price of goods and services over a period of time. The Office for National Statistics, which compiles the official measures of inflation, determines which goods and services to place in an enormous 'basket' of goods and services to calculate inflation. These changes reflect the changing nature of consumers in Britain – for example, it may remove CDs and replace them with subscriptions to online music streaming services to reflect the way consumers enjoy music today. Rising inflation has the effect of reducing the purchasing value of money.

The inflation rate is a measure of the average change over a period, usually 12 months. If inflation is at 4%, this means that the price of products and services is 4% higher than a year earlier, requiring us to spend an extra 4% to buy the same things we bought 12 months ago, and that any savings and investments must generate 4% (after any taxes) to keep pace with inflation. There are two official measures of inflation used by the government – the Consumer Prices Index (CPI) and the Retail Prices Index (RPI). See separate entries in the Jargon Buster for more information.

Inheritance tax (IHT): the tax levied on the total value of your estate after you die, IHT has to be paid by the beneficiaries of your estate before they can receive any of the money from it. There is an IHT threshold – known as the 'nil-rate band' – below which no tax is levied (£325,000 in 2015/16). Any amount above the nil-rate band is subject to tax at 40%.

Interest-only mortgage: a loan in which the borrower pays only the interest on the sum borrowed for the life of the mortgage but, at the end of the mortgage term, still owes what they originally borrowed. The advantage of an interest-only mortgage is that the monthly repayment is much lower than for a comparable repayment mortgage. Lenders insist the borrower also invests in an endowment, Isa, or pension savings policy, which, on maturity, is intended to pay off the capital loan.

Intestacy: if you die without making a will, your estate is subject to the rules of intestacy, which generally mean it is divided up by the state. You should make a will to ensure this doesn't happen.

Isa: individual savings accounts were introduced on 6 April 1999 to replace personal equity plans (Peps) and tax-exempt special savings accounts (Tessas) with one plan that covered both stock market and savings products, the returns from which are tax-exempt. The Isa is not in itself an investment product; rather, it's a tax-free 'wrapper' in which you place investments and savings up to a specified annual allowance on which the returns (capital growth, dividends, interest) are tax-exempt (so you don't have to declare Isas and their contents on your tax return). **New Isa/Nisa:** the single account formed by the merger of cash Isas and stocks-and-shares Isas from 1 July 2014. The maximum annual allowance in the 2015/15 tax year is £15,240 and savers can decide how much to hold in cash or stocks and shares in any combination they like.

Junior Isa: the child version of the Isa, which replaced the Child Trust Fund. They are saving-and-investment wrappers that shield any growth in your children's cash from income and capital gains tax.

Leasehold: the right to hold or use assets (generally property, but also vehicles) for a fixed period of time at a given price, without transfer of ownership, on the basis of a lease contract. Leasehold ownership of a residential property is simply a long tenancy, such as the right to occupation and use of a flat for a specified period. The 'term' of the lease is fixed at the beginning and so decreases in length year by year and the property can be bought and sold during that term. When new, leases are for 99 or 125 years until their eventual expiry, whereupon ownership of the property reverts to the landlord.

Life insurance: insures you for a specific period of time, at a premium fixed by your age, health and the amount the life is insured for. If you die while the policy is in force, the insurance company pays the claim. However, if you survive to the end of the term, or cease paying the premiums, the policy is finished and has no remaining value whatsoever as it has value only if you make a claim. For this reason, life insurance is much cheaper than life assurance (also called 'whole of life').

Loan-to-value (LTV): shows how much of a property is being financed and is also a way of telling how much equity you have in a property. The higher the LTV ratio, the greater the risk for the lender, so borrowers with small deposits or not much equity in the property will be charged higher interest rates than borrowers with large deposits. The LTV ratio is calculated by dividing the loan value by the property value and then multiplying by 100. For example, a £140,000 loan on a £200,000 property has an LTV ratio of 70%.

National Insurance (NI): a scheme originally established in 1944 to provide protection against sickness and unemployment as well as to help fund the National Health Service (NHS) and state benefits. NI contributions are compulsory and based on a person's earnings above a certain threshold. There are several classes of NI but which one an individual pays depends on whether they are employed, self-employed, unemployed or an employer.

Negative equity: the circumstances in which a property is worth less than the outstanding mortgage debt secured on it. Although it traps householders in their properties, the Council of Mortgage Lenders (CML) says there is no causal link between negative equity and mortgage repayment problems. During the housing market recession in 1993, the CML estimated 1.5 million UK households had negative equity but most homeowners sat tight, continued to pay their mortgages and eventually recovered their equity position.

No-claims bonus: a discount on a car insurance premium as a reward for having not made a claim on the policy. The NCB is earned for every year of claim-free driving-up to a maximum of five years (although some insurers may offer discounts for more years). The actual discount on the insurance premium will depend on the insurer. If you make a claim, your insurance company may reduce your discount by a number of years, so you have to 'earn' these over again, or it may revoke the NCB entirely. Motorists can generally transfer their NCB across to another insurer and can pay an additional premium to protect it so that, should they have an accident, the NCB remains intact.

Notice account: a savings account on which the account holder is required to give a period of notice before making a withdrawal or else face a penalty, usually a loss of a specific number of days' interest, or pay a fee.

Offset mortgage: a way of combining a mortgage and savings so the savings 'offset' and reduce the mortgage. Rather than earning interest on savings, the savings reduce the mortgage and the interest paid on the borrowing, so savings are effectively earning interest at a higher rate than most mainstream savings accounts will pay.

Open-ended funds: a collective investment fund that invests in other companies and assets. It gets bigger as more people invest in the fund, while it shrinks as people take their money out.

Overdraft: an agreement with your bank that authorises you to withdraw more funds from your account than you have deposited in it. Many banks charge for this privilege either as a fixed fee or as interest on the money overdrawn at a special high rate. Some banks charge a fee and interest, while others offer a free overdraft but impose very high charges for exceeding the agreed limit of your overdraft.

Packaged account: a current account that charges a monthly fee in return for a 'package' of additional services, such as travel insurance, credit card protection, mobile phone insurance, identity theft insurance, car breakdown cover or a 'concierge service' that will book airline and theatre tickets or restaurant tables. However, many consumer experts say that the features are overpriced, that more competitive deals exist elsewhere in the market and that very few packaged account holders actually take advantage of the features.

Passive/tracker fund: passive funds aim to replicate the performance of an index, such as the FTSE 100. This means that performance will never exceed that of the index it is tracking. However, because they usually require no active management, they tend to be cheaper than active funds.

Payday loans: short-term cash loans designed to be used mid-way through the month to tide the borrower over until they next get paid, whereupon the loan is settled. They are generally used by people with bad credit ratings and/or no access to short-term credit such as an overdraft or credit card. Until recently, this type of borrowing has been hugely expensive, with typical APRs around 2,300%. The industry became regulated in 2014 and the amount lenders could charge in interest and fees was capped at twice the original loan.

Payment protection insurance (PPI): designed to cover you should you fall ill, have an accident or lose your job and be unable to make repayments on loans or credit cards. However, the cover is overpriced and filled with exclusions (policies exclude self-employment, contract employees and pre-existing medical conditions) and was often mis-sold because the exclusions were never fully explained. Banks have paid billions in compensation to victims, and continue to do so – PPI has been the most complained-about product since 2011.

Premium bonds: a type of savings product backed by the government's NS&I organisation, in which you can buy up to £30,000 worth of bonds in return for entry into a monthly prize draw. These prizes (or interest payments) should average out at 1.3%, although you can win up to £1 million, while some people never win at all. You get your capital back intact whenever you want to sell.

Private medical insurance (PMI): allows you to skip the NHS waiting list and arrange treatment at a time you choose. With most PMI policies, you pay a monthly premium (the older you are, generally the higher the premium) and the policy will then pay out, up to specified cover limits and after an agreed excess, for any treatment you might need. Not all conditions are covered by PMI and you get what you pay for: the more cover you want, the higher your premium will be.

Regular savings account: these require customers to deposit money each month, without fail. They come with a number of restrictions, such as monthly deposit limits, no one-off lump sum deposits and restricted withdrawal facilities. Although they are marketed with impressive-looking rates, it's important to remember that, as your money builds up gradually, your overall return will be lower than if you'd deposited a lump sum.

Remortgaging: changing mortgages without moving home. Property owners chiefly remortgage to get a better deal but some do so to release equity in their homes or to finance home improvements, the costs of which are added to the new mortgage. Even though you're not moving house, you still need to engage solicitors for conveyancing and the new lender will require the property to be surveyed and valued.

Repossession: a homeowner's worst nightmare, this is an action of last resort by mortgage lenders to recover money from borrowers who have failed to keep up with repayments on their mortgage or other loan secured on their home. Repossession is a legal procedure that has to go through several processes before the homeowner is evicted and the property repossessed.

RPI: replaced as the official measure of inflation by the Consumer Prices Index (see CPI on page 216) in December 2003, the Retail Prices Index remains another ongoing measure of inflation and includes housing costs.

Sipp: a self-invested personal pension offers a flexible and tax-efficient method of preparing for your retirement. It gives you all sorts of options on how you put money in, how you invest it and how it's paid out, and offers a greater number of investment opportunities than if the fund were managed by a pension company. Sipps are very flexible and allow investments such as quoted and unquoted shares, investment funds, cash deposits, commercial property and intangible property.

Social lending: the name given to a certain type of financial transaction that takes place directly between individuals, or 'peers', without the use of a traditional financial institution such as a bank – hence why it is also called 'peer-to-peer lending' or simply 'P2P'. Various social lending websites incorporate a number of strong risk controls and screen all potential borrowers by checking their credit history. Lenders agree to lend a specific amount for a stated return and lenders' cash is pooled between borrowers, spreading the risk. The major social lending companies are Zopa, RateSetter and Funding Circle.

Stakeholder pension: a form of money purchase (defined contribution) pension that has a minimum set of standards, including low charges. Designed to appeal to people on low and middle incomes who wanted to save for retirement, but for whom existing pension arrangements were either too expensive or unsuitable.

Stamp duty: a hugely unpopular tax paid on property and share purchases. It is charged at 2% on the portion of a property value exceeding £125,000 and up to £250,000. A 5% charge then applies to the portion of value that exceeds £250,000 up to £925,000. Between £925,001 and £1.5 million, the charge is 10% and for everything above £1.5 million, a 12% charge is enforced. As for shares, stamp duty is payable if you have share transfers valued at more than £1,000. The duty is charged at a rate of 0.5%, rounded up to the nearest £5, on each document to be stamped. So £1,995 of shares bought using a single transfer form incur a 0.5% charge of £9.97. This is rounded up to the nearest £5 so the stamp duty paid is £10.

SVR: every mortgage lender has a standard variable rate of interest, or SVR, on which it bases all its mortgage deals, including fixed and discounted rate and tracker mortgages. When special deals come to an end, the terms of the deal usually state that the borrower has to pay the lender's SVR for a period of time or pay redemption penalties. The lender's SVR is, in turn, based on the Bank of England's base lending rate decided by the Bank's Monetary Policy Committee (MPC). Every time the MPC raises its rate, mortgage lenders generally increase their SVR by the same amount but when the MPC lowers its rate, lenders are often slow to pass this on or don't pass on the full cut to borrowers. However, at time of writing, the MPC hadn't raised interest rates from 0.5% since March 2009.

Tax code: used by an employer or pension provider to calculate the amount of tax to deduct from pay or pension. A tax code is usually made up of several numbers followed by a letter. If you replace the letter in your tax code with 'o', you will get the total amount of income you can earn in a year before paying tax, for example 1000L would mean a person could earn up to £10,000 before paying tax.

The wrong tax code could mean a person ends up paying too much or too little tax.

Total expense ratio (TER): a single percentage snapshot of the total cost of your investment, including all fees and charges.

Unsecured loan: a loan that is not secured on any asset you already own, such as a house, car or other assets and so is a riskier prospect for the lender. Therefore, they usually come with higher interest rates than their secured counterparts, are less flexible and levy high redemption penalties. Most personal loans are unsecured.

VAT: invented by a Frenchman in 1954 and introduced in the UK on 1 April 1973, VAT is an indirect tax levied on the value added in the production of goods and services, from primary production to final consumption and is paid by the buyer. Its levying is complex, with a number of exemptions and exclusions. For example, in the UK, VAT is payable on chocolate-covered biscuits, but not on chocolate-covered cakes and the non-VAT status of McVitie's Jaffa Cakes was challenged in a UK court case to determine whether a Jaffa Cake was a cake or a biscuit. The judge ruled that the Jaffa Cake is a cake, McVitie's won the case and VAT is not paid on Jaffa Cakes in the UK. VAT on most goods and services is currently 20%.